Hayate the Combat Butler

14

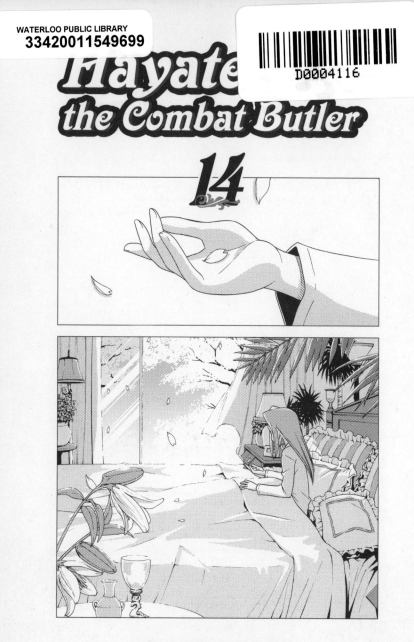

KENJIRO HATA

CONTENTS
MAIN

Episode 1: "No Matter How High the Anticipation of a Great Punch Line, a Boy Must Live Up to a Girl's Expectations"

I JUST REMEMBERED... ISN'T TODAY SAKUYA-SAN'S BIRTHDAY?

HEY, YEAH. SHE'S PROBABLY HAVING A PARTY SOME-WHERE.
THAT'S RIGHT.

AREN'T YOU GOING TO CELEBRATE WITH HER, OJÔ-SAMA?
IT'S HER BIRTH-DAY, AFTER ALL.
...
HM?
BLINK
BLINK
OH... WELL...
...I GUESS I COULD GO...

YOU LOOK A BIT WORN OUT.
HUH?
ER...NO, IT'S NOTHING!!

I'M... JUST ...
...A LITTLE TIRED ...
RUB RUB
WELL, YOU JUST FINISHED YOUR FIRST DAY AT YOUR PART-TIME JOB.

YOU WORKED VERY HARD, SO IT'S NATURAL TO BE TIRED.
Y...YOU THINK SO? YOU REALLY THINK I WORKED HARD?
YES, OF COURSE. YOU DID WELL...

I SEE. WELL, CAN'T DO NOTHIN' 'BOUT IT NOW.
MUR MUR
WELCOME!

SHE SAID SHE'D COME VISIT YOU AFTER HER NAP, BUT...
AW...SHE PROBABLY WON'T WAKE UP 'TIL MORNING. DAT'S OKAY. DON'T PUSH HER.

OKAY, TALK TO YA LATER.
SO LONG! ♡
YAK YAK

WELL, WELL...
KLIK

IN DA END, YER MY ONLY CHILDHOOD FRIEND WHO MADE IT ALL DA WAY HERE.
ISUMI-SAN'S LOST SOMEWHERE AS USUAL.
SHOULDN'T YOU BE MORE CONCERNED ABOUT THAT?

SIGH...DIS IS SAD. IT'S TRUE DERE ARE A LOT OF PEOPLE GATHERED IN DA BALL-ROOM...
...BUT ALL DA PALS WHO'VE BEEN WITH ME SINCE I WAS A KID HAVE LET ME DOWN.

AND ALL I WANT FOR A PRESENT...
PLIP

...IS SOME-THING DAT'LL MAKE ME LAUGH JUST A LITTLE...

OH WELL! SINCE YER DA ONLY CUTE GUY AROUND, YOU'D BETTER BE ***REAL*** FUNNY!

YOU'RE IN A PARTY MOOD ALREADY.

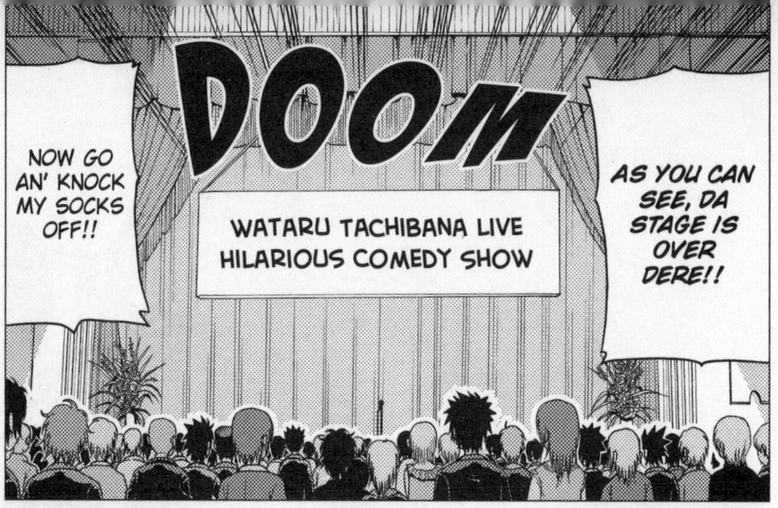
AS YOU CAN SEE, DA STAGE IS OVER DERE!!
DOOM
WATARU TACHIBANA LIVE
HILARIOUS COMEDY SHOW
NOW GO AN' KNOCK MY SOCKS OFF!!

...

HUH?
YAK YAK
BUT...
WOO HOO!
YEAH!
GO ON... KNOCK MY SOCKS OFF!!

BUT... UM...
PLEASE. KNOCK. MY. SOCKS. OFF. ♡ ♡

IS SHE SERIOUS? WHAT FRESH HELL IS THIS? WHAT HAVE I DONE TO DESERVE THIS?
PLEASE TELL ME, GOD...

YOU HAVE A VERY COURAGEOUS FRIEND.
HE WAS A HEROIC WARRIOR IN A PAST LIFE.

WHAT NOW? SHOULD I JUST FORGET THIS AND GO HOME?
BUT I'D BE BETRAYING SAKUYA. STILL, THE MOOD IN THIS ROOM...

WAKA, GIVE IT YOUR BEST!
FRET
FRET

I HAVE NO CHOICE. IF THIS IS MY FATE...
...I'LL DO IT!!

EVERY-BODY IN THE BALL-ROOM!!
WSST

WHOOSH
EYES ON THE STAGE!!
WSST
WOW!!
WHAT'S DAT TECH-NIQUE?

HEY, LOOK AT MY FINGER!
WIGGLE

SHIIING
...
THOSE TEN SECONDS FELT LONGER THAN A YEAR.

CLAP CLAP
CLAP CLAP
CLAP CLAP
CLAP CLAP

THE GUESTS WERE MOVED TO PITY.
YAY!
CLAP
...
CLAP
OHHH
CLAP
BRAVO!

WAKA DID IT!
BUT HOW DID HE DO IT?
SO STRANGE...
SAKI-SAN DECIDED TO ASK HIM HOW HE DID THAT TRICK.

UM...GOOD JOB, GOOD JOB.

YOU WERE TRULY AMAZIN'.

C'MON, DON'T SULK OR NOTHIN'.

JUST KILL ME...

...

...

SIGH

NOW, NOW, DON'T SAY DAT.
YOU WERE COOL.

D...DON'T LIE TO ME...
IT'S TRUE. IF ISUMI HAD SEEN DAT, SHE'D HAVE FALLEN FOR YA ON DA SPOT.

GET SERIOUS! THERE'S NO WAY!
NAH, IT'S TRUE.
waiting room

I REALLY LIKE...
...DAT ABOUT YOU.

...

AW, GEEZ... STOP CLINGING TO ME LIKE WHEN WE WERE KIDS.
WSST
WHOA! DON'T JUMP UP LIKE DAT!!
KYA!!
WHUMP
WATCH IT!!

HUH?

BDMP BDMP BDMP BDM
...
BDMP BDMP BDMP
...

BDMP BDMP
BDMP BDMP
...
BDMP BDMP
BDMP BDMP

SAKUYA LIKES WATARU-KUN... AND WATARU-KUN IS ATTACKING SAKUYA.
WHOA WHOA
YER WRONG!!
YA TALK LIKE YA SAW DA WHOLE THING, BUT IT AIN'T LIKE DAT!!

HUH?
BUT...IF YA *DID* SEE DA WHOLE THING, THEN YA KNOW...

WATARU-KUN ACTUALLY LIKES...ME.
!!
WAIT... THAT'S...
I'M FLATTERED TO HEAR THAT WATARU-KUN LIKES ME...

...BUT THAT STAGE ACT WAS...
TWINKLE
...QUES-TIONABLE.

...
...

IN A LARGE VENUE LIKE THAT, IT'S DIFFICULT FOR THE AUDIENCE TO SEE WHAT YOUR FINGER IS DOING. IT WOULD HAVE BEEN BETTER TO GO WITH A BROADER ACTION, USING YOUR WHOLE BODY.
PANNED BY THE CRITICS!!

SO IF I HAD TO DECIDE ON MY FEELINGS FOR YOU BASED ON...
SLAM
WAIT! I'M GOING BACK UP THERE RIGHT NOW!!
...

WHAT'S WRONG WITH WATARU-KUN?
YA REALLY *ARE* A DEMON, AREN'T YA?

SERIOUSLY... WHAT ARE YOU GUYS UP TO?
HUH?

NAGI!!
I CAME ALL THE WAY HERE FOR *THIS*?
GOOD EVE-NING.
I FIGGERED YA WERE SO TIRED YOU'D BE SLEEPIN' 'TIL MORNING.
I *AM* TIRED!! I *DID* WANT TO SLEEP UNTIL MORNING!!

BUT...
...IT'S YOUR *BIRTHDAY*, ISN'T IT?

SO HERE'S A PRESENT FOR YOU.
...

HEH

THANKS, NAGI.
HMPH... FORGET ABOUT IT.

OJÔ-SAMA WAS SO SLEEPY SHE COULDN'T WALK STRAIGHT, BUT SHE INSISTED...
WATCH IT, HAYATE!!
HA HA...
WELL, WELL... HAYATE-HAN.
HUH?

DA FACT DAT YER HERE MEANS...
...
...YOU'LL BE DOIN' SOMETHIN' *FUNNY* FER ME, RIGHT?

...
HUH?

HAYATE AYASAKI LIVE
LAUGH-A-MINUTE SHOW!!
...

WHAT...
...SHOULD I DO, GOD?

THIS SEEMS PROMISING, SO LET'S KEEP IT GOING INTO THE NEXT EPISODE.
WHAT? YOU JUST RAISED THE BAR AGAIN, AND NOW YOU'RE PUTTING IN A CLIFFHANGER?

Episode 2:
"When You Think About It, Turning into an Animal when Your True Identity Is Revealed Is Scary"

WHEW!
FINALLY DONE!

THANKS FOR YOUR HARD WORK.
I'LL TAKE CARE OF THE CLEANUP.
OKAY, GREAT.

I CAN'T BELIEVE THEY'VE GOT YOU MANAGING THE FRESHMEN WELCOMING CEREMONY ON TOP OF EVERYTHING ELSE.
I KNOW THE SCHOOL'S ADMINISTRATIVE DIRECTOR IS FLAKY, BUT THEY'RE PUTTING TOO MUCH ON OUR SHOULDERS.
IT JUST MEANS THEY TRUST US.
GOOD. LET'S TAKE ADVANTAGE OF THAT TRUST...
...AND SURPRISE THEM BY SELLING OFF THE LAND THE SCHOOL IS BUILT ON.
HEH

HEY, WHERE'S THE SECRE-TARY, CHIHA-RU-SAN, TODAY?
SHE SAID THERE WAS SOMETHING SHE ABSO-LUTELY HAD TO TAKE CARE OF.
I SEE.
WAIT... THAT'S NOT...
JUST KID-DING! ♡

SHE'S MOVING QUICKLY TO SELL THAT LAND...
NO...
I DON'T KNOW WHAT YOU'RE THINKING, BUT TRUST ME, YOU'RE WRONG.

AS FOR WHAT ON EARTH CHIHARU-SAN IS DOING...
HUH?
YA WANT TA KNOW IF NAGI AND HAYATE ARE COMIN'?

I'M SURE THEY ARE. NAGI'S MY CHILDHOOD PAL AN' HAYATE ALWAYS STICKS BY HER.
OH... IS THAT RIGHT?
WHY? DON'T YA WANNA SEE 'EM?
N...NO... THAT'S NOT WHAT I MEAN!!
YAK YAK
WAAH WAAH

HMPH
...
THE GIRL WAS CON-CERNED.
HER IDENTITY WASN'T EXPOSED EARLIER BECAUSE HAYATE AND NAGI DIDN'T KNOW HER WELL...
...BUT IF THEY ALL KEEP RUNNING INTO EACH OTHER, EVENTUALLY THE WORLD WILL LEARN THE TRUTH!
I CAN TO SUPPORT AN ADORABLE AND AMAZING PERSON.

HAKUOU ALLOWS STUDENTS TO TAKE PART-TIME JOBS.
BUT I DON'T THINK PEOPLE OUGHT TO KNOW THAT THE SECRE-TARY OF THE STUDENT COUNCIL WORKS AS A MAID.
I HAVE TO CONSIDER THE IMAGE I PROJECT...
A TYPICAL SCENE WHEN CHIHARU IS AT SCHOOL...
HEY, CHI-CHAN! ♡
LET'S ALL GO OUT FOR KARAOKE AND MAKE SOME NOISE!

AH.
NO THANK YOU. I DISLIKE NOISE.

THE WAY I ACT AT WORK IS SO DIFFERENT FROM MY DIGNIFIED PERSONA AT SCHOOL.
I CAN'T LET MYSELF BE EXPOSED!!

I'M IN TROUBLE...
SIGH
I WONDER WHAT'S WRONG WITH HARU-SAN.
TO EXPLAIN HOW SHE GOT INTO THIS SITUATION IN THE FIRST PLACE...
...WE HAVE TO TURN BACK THE CLOCK A BIT!!
POP?
HIS COMPANY WENT BANKRUPT JUST LIKE THAT?
THIS IS NOTHING TO JOKE ABOUT, CHIHARU-CHAN!!
I WASN'T TRYING TO BE FUNNY, MOM...
...BUT LET'S NOT PANIC. I'LL TAKE UP A PART-TIME JOB OR SOMETHING. LET ME HANDLE IT.
YOU'RE SO HEARTLESS, CHIHARU-CHAN!! YOUR POOR MOTHER HAS NEVER HAD TO WORK BEFORE...
SIGH ...
WHAT SHOULD I DO?

WELL, IF I HAVE TO WORK, I'D LIKE IT TO BE SOMETHING FUN.
LIKE A JOB WITH A CUTE UNIFORM.
WREEN
SOMETHING CUTE AND CHALLENGING AND...
WREEN
WAIT, WHAT AM I SAYING?
I CAN'T BE PICKY AT A TIME LIKE THIS!
ZEGA
PIOP
HM...
BUT WHY NOT HAVE A LITTLE FUN?
WELCOME, SIR! CARE TO VISIT OUR NEW MAID CAFÉ?
!
A MAID CAFÉ, HUH?
THE UNIFORMS ARE REALLY CUTE!
HM...
YES, THE UNIFORMS ARE CUTE, BUT...
TICK
TOCK

...IT'S ALL WRONG!!
THEY'RE NOT DOING IT RIGHT!! NOT AT ALL!!

THEY'RE TOO STIFF AND RIGID! THEY AREN'T BRINGING OUT THE CUTENESS OF THE MAID UNIFORM!!
TICK
TOCK
MAID CAFÉ SUNFLOWER
ONCE THEY PUT ON THAT UNIFORM, THEY SHOULD ACT CHEERFUL AND BUBBLY!!
DARN IT!! IF THEY'D JUST LET ME DO IT, I'D MAKE THAT UNIFORM SHINE! IF THEY'D LET ME... LET ME...
MAID CAFÉ SUNFLOWER OPENS TODAY
WOULD YOU LIKE TO WORK AT OUR CAFÉ? WE'RE IN NEED OF A CUTE, CHEERFUL MAID-SAN!! HOURLY RATE: 950 YEN OR MORE* *CHANCE FOR A QUICK RAISE DEPENDING ON PERFORMANCE PLEASE CONTACT

IS...IS THIS A "HELP WANTED" SIGN?
IT... IT CAN'T BE!! IS THIS A SIGN FROM ABOVE?
MAID CAFÉ SUNFLOWER
OPENS TODAY
WOULD YOU LIKE TO WORK AT OUR CAFÉ? WE'RE IN NEED OF A CUTE, CHEERFUL MAID-SAN!! HOURLY RATE: 950 YEN OR MORE*
BUT I'M THE HAKUOU STUDENT COUNCIL SECRETARY!! AND I'M THE IMAGE OF PROPRIETY AT HAKUOU!!
IF ANYONE FROM SCHOOL FINDS OUT I'M WORKING PART-TIME AT A MAID CAFÉ...

HEY!! COME TO THINK OF IT, NOW THAT MY FATHER'S COMPANY HAS GONE BANKRUPT, THERE'S NO WAY HE CAN AFFORD TO KEEP ME AT HAKUOU!
BUT THEN AGAIN...
SO WHO CARES?

EXCUSE ME... ARE YOU HERE ABOUT THE PART-TIME MAID JOB?
YES, PLEASE CONSIDER ME!!
WHAT?
DAD'S COMPANY ISN'T GOING BANKRUPT AFTER ALL?

THEY FOUND AN ANGEL INVESTOR!! SO OUR LITTLE CHIHARU CAN KEEP GOING TO HAKUOU!
...
I GUESS THAT'S GOOD ...
THIS... IS A PROBLEM ...
ONE OF THE REASONS I TOOK THE JOB AS SAKUYA-SAN'S MAID WAS THAT IT WAS MORE DISCREET THAN WORKING AT THE CAFÉ.
I NEVER IMAGINED SHE WAS FRIENDS WITH THOSE TWO... I REALLY SLIPPED UP.

AH... NAGI CAN'T COME, SO YOU AIN'T COMIN' EITHER, HAYATE?
!

NAGI-SAN AND HER BUTLER AREN'T COMING TO YOUR PARTY?
NOPE. NAGI'S TUCKERED OUT AN' TAKIN' A NAP.
IN DA END, YER MY ONLY CHILDHOOD FRIEND WHO MADE IT...
...

WHEW! ♡ I DON'T HAVE TO WORRY ABOUT RUNNING INTO ANYONE I KNOW...
...SO I CAN CONCENTRATE ON WORK. ♡

I SHOULD ACT BUBBLIER THAN USUAL SO THAT SAKUYA-SAN WON'T FEEL BAD ABOUT HER FRIENDS STANDING HER UP... ♡
UM...
HOW MAY I HELP YOU, DEAR GUEST? ♡♡
I'LL GO TOTALLY OVER THE TOP ***LIKE THIS***! ♡

...
...

AIKA-SAN?
WHY IS AIKA-SAN HERE?

CALM DOWN! DON'T PANIC!!
MAYBE SHE HASN'T SEEN THROUGH MY DISGUISE!
W... WELCOME ...

WHAT ARE YOU DOING HERE, CHIHARU-SAN?
SHE KNOWS!!

C... COME NOW, DEAR GUEST.
WHAT ARE YOU SAYING?

YOU MUST HAVE MISTAKEN ME FOR SOMEONE ELSE!
I'M ...
CHIHARU HAYAKAZE. YOU'RE A SOPHOMORE AT HAKUOU GAKUIN, WHERE YOU'RE THE STUDENT COUNCIL SECRETARY.
YOU'RE 16, RESERVED, AND YOU USUALLY WEAR GLASSES.
...
RIGHT? ♡

NO!! IT'S NOT WHAT YOU THINK, AIKA-SAN!! IT'S...
HMM... SO THIS IS WHAT YOU DO IN YOUR SPARE TIME.
I SEE...
THAT'S QUITE A CUTE LOOK FOR YOU. ♡
OH NO!! AIKA-SAN'S EYES TELL ME SHE'S SWITCHED INTO **SADISTIC MODE!!** I'M DOOMED!!

WHAT ARE YOU DOING HERE, AIKA-SAN?
ME? FAMILY DUTY.

THE "AI" IN "AIKA" IS TAKEN FROM THE AIZAWAS, A FAMILY TO WHICH WE ARE INDEBTED.
WHAT? WHO CARES?
I'M NOT ASKING FOR YOUR LIFE STORY HERE!!

BUT CHIHARU-SAN...
...THIS REALLY IS QUITE DIFFERENT FROM THE WAY YOU ACT AT SCHOOL.
BDMP
AH!! WELL... ER...

PLEASE KEEP THIS SECRET FROM THE PRESIDENT AND EVERYONE ELSE.
I'M BEGGING YOU, FORGET YOU EVER SAW THIS...
HA! ♡ I KNOW... ♡

...YOU WOULDN'T BE DRESSED UP LIKE THAT...
...UNLESS YOU HAD A GOOD REASON, CHIHARU-SAN.

AI...AIKA-SAN...
THAT'S WHY...
REVIEW
GRADE CLASS NAME

...I'LL FORGET ALL ABOUT THIS. ♡
SHE'S NOT FORGETTING ABOUT IT!
THIS GIRL HAS NO INTENTION OF FOR-GETTING ANY-THING!!!
LIST OF WEAKNESSES

HEY, HARU-SAN. WATARU'S GONNA START THE SHOW!
YES, MA'AM! I'LL BE THERE IN A MOMENT!!
LET'S TALK ABOUT THIS LATER!!
YES, YES. YOU'D BETTER RUN ALONG.

HMM.
WHAT AN INTERESTING DISCOVERY...
AH!! WEL-COME!!
WELCOME TO THE MANSION!!
!
SERIOUSLY... CAN'T SHE EVER JUST HAVE A MODEST COCKTAIL PARTY OR SOMETHING?
I'VE GOT TO SAY, IT'S PRETTY AMAZING.
WELCOME! WELCOME!

YOU'RE AYASAKI-KUN, AREN'T YOU?
HUH?

THE ONE ALWAYS LOOKING AFTER THE PRESIDENT.
HUH?
ER...
I'M AIKA KASUMI, VICE PRESIDENT OF THE HAKUOU GAKUIN STUDENT COUNCIL.
PLEASED TO MEET YOU, HAYATE AYASAKI-KUN.

AH, YOU'RE THE VICE PRESIDENT AT HAKUOU!! YES, I REALLY APPRECIATE HOW HINAGIKU-SAN ALWAYS LOOKS AFTER ME.
NOT AT ALL. GOOD EVENING TO YOU TOO, SANZENIN-SAN.
HUH? YEAH, HI.

BY THE WAY, WHERE'S SAKUYA?
OH, SAKUYA-SAN IS WITH CHIHARU...

...

SORRY.
SHE'S A LITTLE BUSY RIGHT NOW. YOU SHOULD GIVE HER A MOMENT.
PLEASE WAIT A LITTLE WHILE.
WHEN SAKUYA-SAN IS FREE, I'LL GET HER FOR YOU.
OH, OKAY.

...

HEY!! UMM... AIKA-SAN...
OH, CHIHARU-SAN.

HARU-SAN, I'M HEADIN' FER WATARU'S WAITIN' ROOM!
AH!! I'LL GO WITH YOU!!
WELL, THEN... UM...
SAKUYA-SAN, I WOULD LIKE TO HAVE A LITTLE TALK WITH YOUR MAID-SAN. MAY I BORROW HER?
HUH?
SURE, I DON'T MIND.

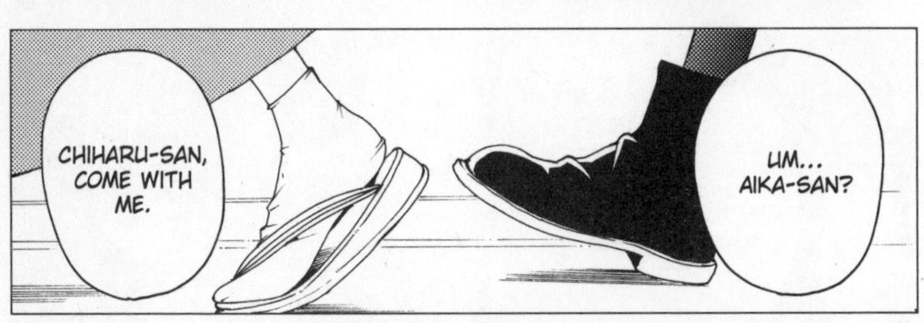
UM... AIKA-SAN?
CHIHARU-SAN, COME WITH ME.

Waiting room
FOR
MS. SANZENIN
NOK
NOK
THIS IS AIKA. SAKUYA-SAN HAS GONE TO WATARU-SAMA'S WAITING ROOM.
OH, OKAY! THANKS!

KA-CHAK
HUH? WHERE'D THE VICE PRESIDENT GO?
YOU GOT ME. MAYBE THE BATHROOM?

BY THE WAY, WHAT'S AIKA-SAN LIKE?
BEATS ME.
I DON'T REALLY KNOW HER, BUT HINA SAYS SHE'S SMART...
...AND VERY KIND.
I SEE...

I'M BEGGING YOU, PLEASE DON'T TELL ANYONE AT SCHOOL ABOUT THIS!!
I TOLD YOU...
...I'D KEEP IT A SECRET.
WHAT'S THAT? THE CLIFF-HANGER FROM THE LAST EPISODE?
...
WELL, WE RAN OUT OF PAGES, SO LET'S CONTINUE THAT NEXT TIME...

Episode 3:
"Where We're Headed To"

...AND THAT'S WHAT HAPPENED. ☆

OHOHOH
AHAHAHA

THEN GEORGE SAID...
...HEY, HEY, THAT'S JUST LIKE *OUR* PRESIDENT!

RIGHT? ☆

HAYATE AYASAKI LIVE LAUGH-A-MINUTE SHOW!!

WHOOOOO!

YEAH!

WOW!

COOL! COOL!

HAYATE-KUN IS AMAZING.
YEAH.
HOW CAN HE SPEAK SO COMFORTABLY IN FRONT OF DAT MANY PEOPLE?
I DON'T CARE FOR HIS CHOICE OF SUBJECT MATTER, THOUGH...
HA HA HA HA HA HA HA HA HA!

WELL? HOW WAS YOUR FIRST DAY WORKING HERE?

OH, I LEARNED A LOT.
I ENJOYED IT VERY MUCH.
IS THAT SO?
I'M GLAD TO HEAR IT.
CAFÉ ACORN

BUT WE HARDLY HAD ANY CUSTOM-ERS AT ALL.
IS THAT OKAY?
HM?
WELL, NOT REALLY, BUT...
...THIS SHOP IS KIND OF A HOBBY FOR ME.

ANYWAY, YOU COULD'VE GONE HOME WITH AYASAKI-KUN AND THE OTHERS. THERE WAS NO NEED FOR YOU TO STAY UNTIL CLOSING.
NO, DON'T WORRY ABOUT ME.
HAYATE-KUN DID MOST OF THE WORK MANAGING THE SHOP.
I WASN'T MUCH HELP AT ALL... SO I FEEL LIKE I SHOULD DO THIS MUCH.

I SEE.

YOU'RE A VERY GOOD PERSON, AYUMU-CHAN.

NO!! I'M NOTHING SPECIAL!!

YOU'RE EMBARRASSING ME!!!

BESIDES, I'D LIKE TO GET REALLY GOOD AT THIS...

...FOR HAYATE-KUN.

CAFÉ ACORN
WELL, I'M GOING UPSTAIRS TO ORGANIZE THE SALES SLIPS.
YOU CAN FINISH CLEANING UP IF YOU LIKE.
OF COURSE! ☆ LEAVE IT TO ME!!
CAFÉ ACORN

DUM DEEDUM DUM

IN ANY CASE...
...WORKING WITH HAYATE-KUN SURE IS DIFFERENT.
CAF

SPARKLE
!!

IT'S SURPRISINGLY HARD TO PREDICT...
...WHAT WILL HAPPEN NEXT.

KLANG

OH, SORRY.
WE'RE ALREADY CLOSED...

EH?

HUH?

EH?

WHAT?
DARN. I WAS HEADING TO THE KITCHEN TO BREW SOME MILK TEA FOR OJÔ-SAMA...
...BUT SOME-HOW I ENDED UP IN A COMPLETELY DIFFERENT WING.

HUH?
FRET
FRET

WHAT'S WRONG?

ARE YOU LOST...
...LIKE ME?
...
AH...

DONCHA TALK TA US ALL CASUAL LIKE DAT.
EAT DIRT, BALDY!

...

UMM...
HELP!! BAD TOUCH!! HELP, POLICE!
HUH? WAIT!! HOLD ON!!
NOOOOO!! HE'S GONNA KIDNAP MEEE...

WHAT'S WITH ALL DA NOISE, Y'INS?
WHAP
!!

WHADDYA DOIN', ASATO? YA FOOL!!

DON'T ASK **ME** WHAT I'M DOIN', HINATA!! **YER** DA ONE MAKIN' TROUBLE FOR FOLKS AGAIN!!

SHUT UP!! JUST DROP DEAD, YA FOOL!!

WHAT DID YA SAY? YER DA ONE WHO SHOULD DIE, DUMMY!!

...

UMM ...

OH, YER STILL HERE?
WHAT A DIMWIT.
...

HA HA HA... DON'T YOU TWO BOTHER THE GUESTS, NOW.
EH?
I'M SORRY. THE CHILDREN ARE GIVING YOU A HARD TIME...

ER...NO ...IT'S OKAY...
YOUR PERFORMANCE EARLIER WAS AMAZING, AYASAKI-KUN.
IT'S BEEN QUITE A WHILE SINCE I LAUGHED SO MUCH.
OH... WELL ...
THANK YOU VERY MUCH.

THAT PART ABOUT THE GREEN ONION THIEF WAS TERRIFIC.
WHO WOULD'VE GUESSED GEORGE WAS FROM AMERICA'S WEST COAST?

HUH?
WAS THERE A BIT LIKE THAT?

...
...
NO, THERE WASN'T.
WHAT'S WITH THIS GUY?

WELL, I NEVER EXPECTED TO MEET YOU HERE, HINA-SAN...

THAT'S *MY* LINE.
WHY ARE YOU WORKING AT THIS PLACE?
LET ME TELL YOU, THIS CAFÉ IS IN THE RED. IT COULD GO UNDER AT ANY MOMENT.
YEAH... I KIND OF GOT THAT IMPRESSION WORKING HERE TODAY.

BUT I'M REALLY ENJOYING THE JOB. NAGI-CHAN AND HAYATE-KUN ARE WORKING HERE TOO. ♡
!
...
HUH?
NAGI... AND HAYATE-KUN?
YES! ♡ ALL THREE OF US WORKED TOGETHER TODAY! ♡

THIS HAS TO BE, LIKE, FATE OR SOMETHING, RIGHT?
I'M REALLY GETTING MY HOPES UP...
...

FOR SOME REASON, SEEING HOW CUTE YOU ARE...
...MAKES ME WANT TO SUPPORT YOUR EFFORTS.
EH?
HINA-SAN...
WHILE I DON'T THINK LOVE IS SOMETHING THAT SHOULDN'T BE SUPPORTED BY OTHERS...
YES...
UMM... DOES IT HAVE TO BE HERE?
WAAH
BLA
BLA
WAAAH

RIGHT... I CAN'T RUN AWAY FROM THIS ANY LONGER...

UMM ...
YES?

SINCE ...
...CHERRY BLOSSOM SEASON IS ALMOST OVER...

...WOULD YOU LIKE TO GO OUT WITH ME TONIGHT...
...AND VIEW THE CHERRY BLOSSOMS?

WHILE WE'RE THERE, I HAVE SOMETHING...
...KIND OF IMPORTANT TO TELL YOU.
...

SO YOU'RE SAKUYA-SAN'S FATHER, AND THE KIDS ARE HER BROTHER AND SISTER?

YEAH. MY NANNY AN' TWO SISTERS ARE HERE TOO, BUT DEY GOT A LITTLE WORN OUT TODAY, SO DEY'RE SLEEPIN' RIGHT NOW.
OH, IS THAT SO?
THAT'S RIGHT, HAYATE-KUN.
BUT I THOUGHT I HEARD...
...YOUR FAMILY HAD ANOTHER PERSON NAMED GILBERT, AN ILLEGITIMATE OLDER BROTHER ON YOUR FATHER'S SIDE...

...
HM?
HM?
HUH?
...

AYASAKI-KUN ...YOU'RE STILL YOUNG...
...SO YOU MAY NOT UNDERSTAND YET...

...BUT A FOREIGN COUNTRY ...
...IS FULL OF TERRIBLE TEMPTATIONS.

...

OH...
THIS MAN IS HOPE-LESS!!
AND SO THE NIGHT OF APRIL 3RD DEEP-ENS...

Episode 4:
"Even in a Samurai Drama, a Person Usually Becomes Obedient when He Sees a Tattoo of Streaming Cherry Blossoms"

WOW!

THE CHERRY BLOSSOMS ARE STILL IN FULL BLOOM!
YES, THEY'RE HANGING IN THERE SURPRISINGLY WELL.

I THOUGHT THE CHERRY BLOSSOMS IN SHIMODA WERE BEAUTIFUL, BUT THE ONES IN TOKYO ARE NICE TOO.
REMEMBER THE CHERRY-BLOSSOM VIEWING PARTY?

ANYWAY...
...I WANTED TO TELL YOU...
AH!! I JUST REMEM-BERED!!

DID YOU KNOW THERE'S A MAJOR LAND-MARK...
...NEAR HERE ON GINKGO SHOPPING STREET?
HUH?

REALLY? I'VE NEVER HEARD ABOUT ANY LANDMARK...
IS THERE SUCH A THING?
YES! JUST PAST THIS PARK!

IS IT OKAY IF WE CHECK IT OUT?

I'VE HEARD THAT IT GIVES PEOPLE COURAGE.

I SEE.

ALL RIGHT.

MAYBE THAT'S THE RIGHT PLACE TO TELL HER.

THERE IT IS! ♡ THE SYMBOL OF THE DISTRICT!

HYOOO
GINGKO'S SUPER FERRIS WHEEL!!
ISN'T IT AMAZING? IT'S OVER 100 METERS TALL! ♡
I DIDN'T KNOW THERE WAS ANYTHING LIKE THIS AROUND HERE!
...

AH... YES...
I... I DIDN'T KNOW ANYTHING ABOUT IT...
NOTE: SHE'S AFRAID OF HEIGHTS.
TWITCH

WELL, HINA-SAN? LET'S TAKE IT FOR A SPIN!!
ALL THE WAY TO THE TOP!!
!

...
ER...
NOTE: SHE'S **VERY** AFRAID OF HEIGHTS.

B... BUT...
UMM... I HAVE SOMETHING IMPORTANT TO TELL YOU...
IN THAT CASE, ALL THE BETTER!!
IT'S EASIER TO TALK WHERE WE CAN BE ALONE!!
FLAP FLAP
COME ON!!
HURRY UP, HINA-SAN!!
...

ER...
ALL RIGHT...
"THIS IS DIVINE VENGEANCE," THOUGHT HINAGIKU (HAVE WE MENTIONED SHE'S AFRAID OF HEIGHTS?).

YOU REALLY *ARE* RICH, AREN'T YOU, SAKUYA-SAN?

AHA!
I GET IT. I DON'T LOOK LIKE A RICH OJÔ-SAMA TO YA, HUH?
NO!! I DIDN'T MEAN IT THAT WAY!!

IT'S JUST THAT YOU WERE ABLE TO RENT THIS HUGE VENUE AND INVITE SO MANY PEOPLE.
AND YOU HAVE A CUTE MAID ALL TO YOURSELF.
IT'S PRETTY IMPRESSIVE.

WHAT'S DAT ABOUT A CUTE MAID? DON'T TELL ME YA GOT A *THING* FOR HARU-SAN...
ER...NO, NO! WHAT'RE YOU SAYING?

HMM...
WELL, DAT'S OKAY.

IT'S ONLY NATURAL THAT DA IMMORTAL, INVINCIBLE AN' UNFLAPPABLE SANZENIN FAMILY BUTLER...
...WOULD BE POPULAR WITH DA LADIES. JUS' DON'T BREAK TOO MANY HEARTS.
WHAT? THAT'S NOT TRUE!!

I...
I'M NOT GOOD...
...WITH GIRLS.

EVEN IF I DID LOVE SOMEONE, I COULDN'T...
ENOUGH ALREADY!! IF THAT'S THE CASE, YOU'RE ON YOUR OWN!!

I'VE HAD ENOUGH OF YOU...
...HAYATE!!

...

WHAT'S WRONG? YA GOT QUIET ALL OF A SUDDEN...
SORRY! JUST A QUICK FLASH-BACK!!

WELL, IF YER REALLY INTERESTED, IN A FEW MINUTES I'LL SHOW YA JUST HOW WEALTHY I AM.
HUH?

BY THE WAY... I AIN'T SEEN NAGI IN A WHILE.
OJÔ-SAMA WAS READY TO COLLAPSE, SO SHE SAID SHE'D LIE DOWN FOR A BIT. SHE'S NAPPING WITH MARIA-SAN.

OH, IS DAT SO?
YES.
HAYATE-KUN!

!
HAVE YOU SEEN NAGI?

MEAN-WHILE...
WOW! THIS IS AMAZING! ♡

LOOK, HINA-SAN!! LOOK!!
WHAT AN INCREDIBLE PANORAMA!
UM... HINA-SAN?
YES, IT'S AMAZING.
I'VE NEVER SEEN SUCH AN INCREDIBLE VIEW.
SIGH

UMM... I REALLY DON'T THINK YOU CAN SEE IT WITH YOUR EYES CLOSED...
N-NO PROBLEM!! I DO KENDO, SO I CAN SEE EVERYTHING THROUGH MY MIND'S EYE!!
BUT DON'T YOU WANT TO LOOK AT THE VIEW THROUGH YOUR *REGULAR* EYES?

OH, HINA-SAN...
...ARE YOU AFRAID OF HEIGHTS?
!

N-NO WAY!!
I'M NOT A LITTLE CHILD!! I'M NOT ACROPHOBIC!!
WHAT DOES BEING A CHILD HAVE TO DO WITH IT?

J-JUST WATCH ME!! I'M NOT AFRAID TO LOOK!!
WHY, I'LL EVEN...
...LOOK ...
...DOWN...
IT'S...NO... PROBLEM... NO PROBLEM... AT ALL...
READY TO FAINT.
SHE'S AFRAID OF HEIGHTS, ALL RIGHT.

THE WAY SHE'S ACTING...
...REMINDS ME OF SOMEONE.
SOME-ONE WHO HATES TO LOSE...
THAT'S IT!
SHE'S JUST LIKE NAGI-CHAN!

YEAH, THOSE TWO...
...ARE SO CUTE THAT WAY.

KLUNK
HUH? WE STOPPED.
!!
PLIP PLIP
WHOA!!
HINA-SAN! CALM DOWN!!
ARE WE... GOING TO DIE?
DON'T WORRY!! WE'LL BE FINE!!
IT JUST STOPPED FOR A BIT, THAT'S ALL!!

I SEE.
WE'LL LAUNCH THE GREAT NAGI SANZENIN OJÔ-SAMA SEARCH AND RESCUE MISSION ASAP.

THERE APPEAR TO BE NO SIGNS OF KIDNAPPING. BECAUSE THE AIZAWA FAMILY'S DIGNITY IS AT STAKE...
...WE'LL LET THIS SMALL, ELITE TEAM DEAL WITH THE SITUATION. THE YOUNGER CHILDREN ARE IN BED.
SOME ELITE TEAM.
TO BEGIN WITH, I'VE SET TRAPS LIKE THIS...
...ALL OVER THE BUILDING.

NAGI-CHAN LOVES MANGA, SO WHEN SHE PICKS UP THE BOOK LIKE THIS...
WSST
SNAP

DA FUTURE OF DA AIZAWA FAMILY LOOKS BLEAK.
SO AS NOT TA WASTE DAD'S ULTIMATE SACRIFICE ...
...WE HAFTA FIND NAGI AT ANY COST.

BUT THIS PLACE IS *HUGE.*
HOW ARE WE GOING TO FIND HER?

LEMME SEE. WE COULD METHODI-CALLY GATHER INFORMA-TION...
SEARCH EVERY ROOM WIT' A FINE-TOOTH COMB...
HOLD ON...

UMM...
WHAT'S UP, ISUMI-SAN?

FIRST OF ALL...
TWINKLE
...WE SHOULD CALL NAGI'S CELL PHONE.

TWINKLE

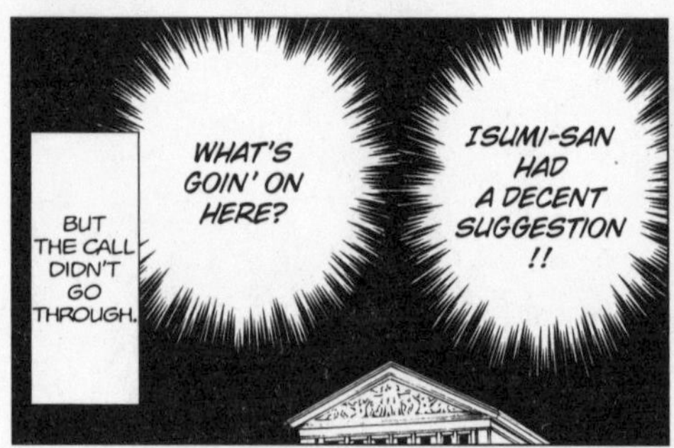
ISUMI-SAN HAD A DECENT SUGGESTION!!
WHAT'S GOIN' ON HERE?
BUT THE CALL DIDN'T GO THROUGH.

AT A TIME LIKE THIS...
...JUST SING A SONG. ♡

...
SNIFF
A SONG?

I USED TO HAVE A PRIVATE TUTOR...
...AND HE TOLD ME THAT WHEN YOU'RE IN TROUBLE, JUST SING A SONG.
IT'S STRANGE, BUT HE NEVER TUTORED ME IN SCHOOL SUBJECTS.
ALL HE DID WAS SHOW ME HOW TO PLAY THE GUITAR...

THAT'S NOT JUST STRANGE... THAT'S ***MESSED UP***.
YES. BUT HE WAS REALLY FUNNY AND I LIKED HIM A LOT... AND I STILL TREASURE THE GUITAR HE GAVE ME WHEN WE PARTED. ♡
I SEE...

BUT MAYBE HE'S RIGHT.
MAYBE A SONG...

O-OKAY...
...PLEASE SING WITH ME.
SURE! ♡

HERE I GO...
AHEM

DANGO, DANGO... ♪
THREE IN A ROW, DANGO, DANGO... ♫
DANGO ON A STICK, DANGO, DANGO... ♪

WOW, YOU'RE ACTUALLY SINGING.
SNAP
!!

WAIT!! WHAT DO YOU MEAN?
AND YOUR CHOICE OF SONG IS A LITTLE QUESTIONABLE FOR A TEENAGE GIRL...
I...I CAN'T HELP IT!! IT WAS THE ONLY SONG I COULD THINK OF!!

ANYWAY, IT WAS *YOUR* IDEA TO SING A SONG, AYUMU!!!
WHY DIDN'T YOU SING ALONG?
OKAY, OKAY... I JUST THOUGHT IT MIGHT...

...DISTRACT YOU A LITTLE.
!
...
HOW DO YOU FEEL?
...

THAT... THAT WASN'T FAIR.
DON'T SAY THAT.

VRRRR

WELL, IT'S ABOUT TIME...
...I HEARD THIS IMPORTANT THING YOU HAD TO TELL ME.

Episode 5: "Distance—Even if It's Near"

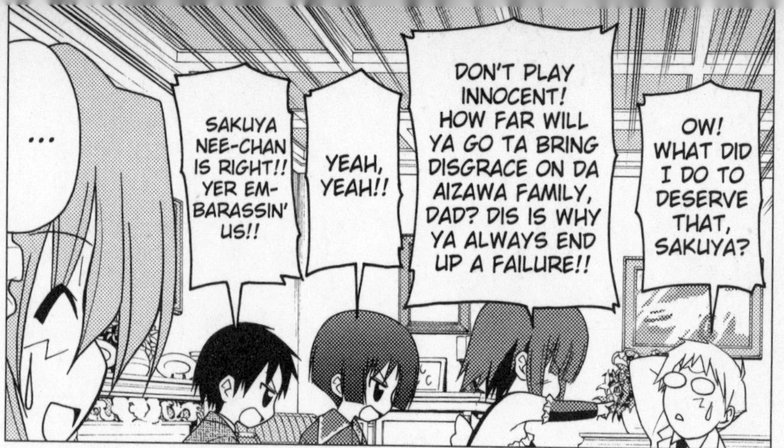

...

?!

WHAT'S WRONG?

SHF

I'M KIND OF WIPED OUT.

I'M GOING TO TAKE A NAP.

Episode 5:
"Distance—Even if It's Near"

FOR A LONG TIME...
...I'VE WANTED TO APOLOGIZE TO YOU FOR SOME-THING...
APOLO-GIZE?

HA HA!
WHAT ARE YOU SAYING, HINA-SAN?
I'M THE ONE WHO'S ALWAYS CAUSING TROUBLE FOR *YOU*. WHAT WOULD YOU HAVE TO APOLOGIZE ABOUT?

IT'S ABOUT HAYATE-KUN.
HUH?

ANYWAY, I WONDER WHERE OJÔ-SAMA IS.

HMM... I KINDA UNDER-STAND HOW SHE FEELS...
HUH?

HOW DO I PUT DIS? SHE TENDS TA GET LONELY A LOT, SO SHE...

DAT REMINDS ME. YER PARENTS ARE STILL ALIVE, RIGHT?
WELL, PROB-ABLY.
THEY'RE PRETTY TENA-CIOUS.

I'VE BEEN MEANING TA ASK YA FOR A WHILE NOW...
ASK ME WHAT?

IF YER PARENTS CLEANED UP THEIR ACT...
...AND TOLD YA THEY WANTED Y'INS TA LIVE TOGETHER AGAIN...

...WHAT WOULD YA DO?
...

HEH... I DON'T HAVE TO WORRY ABOUT THAT...
...BECAUSE THERE'S NO WAY IT'LL EVER HAPPEN.
WOW, YA DON'T SEEM BOTH-ERED ABOUT DAT.

WELL, I CAN'T GIVE THEM ANOTHER CHANCE. NOT AGAIN.
AGAIN?

I DO THINK THAT SOME-DAY...
...I'D LIKE...
...TO FIND MY ***OLDER BROTHER***, THOUGH.

HUH? YA GOT A BIG BROTHER?
YES.
HE'S MUCH OLDER THAN ME, THOUGH.

IS DAT SO? HMM...I SEE...
?
WHAT'S WRONG?

NOTHIN'... UM...IT'S JUST...
...S-SINCE WE'RE ALONE, I WANTED TA TELL YA SOMETHIN'...
YES?

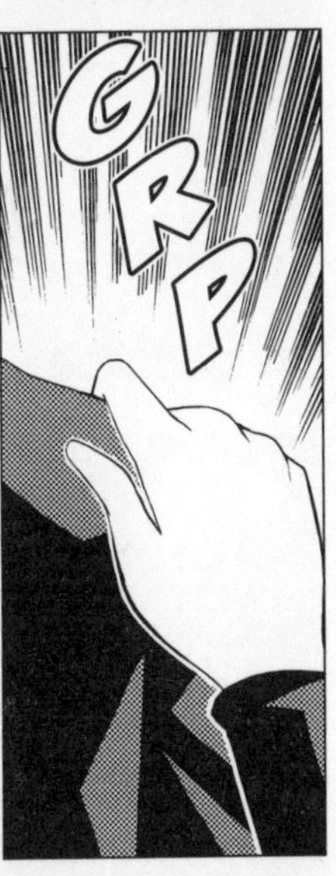
GRP

TO TELL YA THE TRUTH, I...
I SORTA GOT DIS ***LONGIN'*** TO HAVE A BIG BROTHER.
HUH?

UMM...
SAKUYA-SAN, IF I REMEMBER CORRECTLY, YOU ***DO*** HAVE A BIG BROTHER. GILBERT, RIGHT?
THAT'S NOT DA KINDA BIG BROTHER I GOT IN MIND!! I DON'T WANNA CATEGORIZE ***DAT*** AS MY BIG BROTHER!!
UM...

*"Big Brother Hayate."

SHE USED TA LOOK AT DA STARS WITH NAGI.

SO WHENEVER NAGI FEELS LONESOME, SHE ALWAYS WANDERS OFF ALONE TA...

OJÔ-
SAMA!!

OH, HAYATE.

I'VE BEEN LOOKING FOR YOU.
WHAT ARE YOU DOING ALL BY YOURSELF?

UM... WELL...
...IT'S NO BIG DEAL, BUT...

...MAYBE IT'S BECAUSE THIS YEAR, IN SHIMODA...
...THE MEMORIES CAME BACK STRONGER THAN USUAL.

WHILE I WAS WATCHING SAKUYA'S FAMILY...
...I FELT JUST A LITTLE...

...LIKE BEING PART OF A FAMILY...
...WOULDN'T BE SO BAD...

YOU KNOW, FAMILIES AREN'T ALWAYS SO RELIABLE.
LOOK AT MY PARENTS.

HA HA...
YOU'RE RIGHT.
ANYWAY...

...IF YOU WANT A FAMILY, THERE'S MARIA-SAN...
...AND ME.

...

A...LITTLE WHILE BACK...

...A MAN WHO TOLD ME HE'D STAY BY MY SIDE AND ALWAYS PROTECT ME...
...WENT AWAY, JUST LIKE THAT.

MY MOTHER LEFT ME...
...AND SOMEDAY MARIA WILL TOO.
AS YOU ALWAYS FIND THAT STAR WHEN YOU LOOK TO THE SKY, NO MATTER WHAT HAPPENS...
MOTHER IS THE SKY ITSELF, INCLUDING ALL THE STARS...
SO, I'LL BE WATCHING OVER YOU, FOREVER.
BUT MOTHER...
HM?

SURE, MARIA'S WITH ME FOR NOW, AND SHE'S LIKE FAMILY TO ME...
...BUT SOMEDAY SHE'LL FALL IN LOVE WITH SOMEONE...
...AND SHE WON'T WANT TO HANG AROUND LOOKING AFTER ME ALL THE TIME.

AND I THINK THAT DAY...
...ISN'T SO FAR OFF.

...
OJÔ-SAMA...

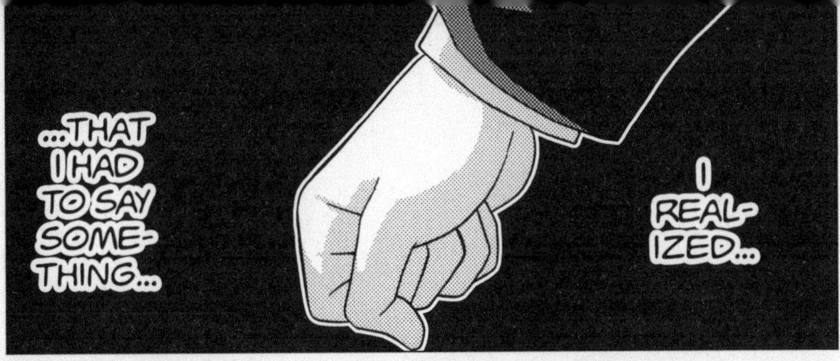
I REAL-IZED...
...THAT I HAD TO SAY SOME-THING...

...TO THIS LITTLE GIRL ...
...WHO LOOKED SO LONELY.
I HAD TO SAY SOMETHING...
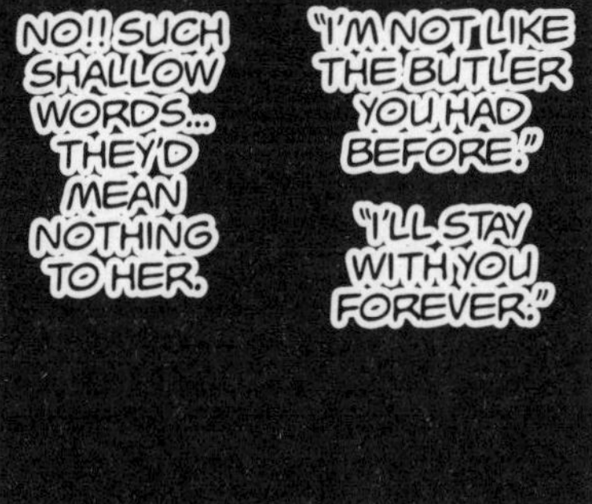
"I'M NOT LIKE THE BUTLER YOU HAD BEFORE."
"I'LL STAY WITH YOU FOREVER."
NO!! SUCH SHALLOW WORDS... THEY'D MEAN NOTHING TO HER.

THERE HAD TO BE SOME-THING I COULD SAY.
SOMETHING THAT WOULD RESONATE WITH HER... AND ERASE OJÔ-SAMA'S LONELINESS... SOMETHING...

OJÔ-SAMA!!

HEY!
LOOK AT MY FINGER!
WIGGLE

WHAM
HOW STUPID CAN YOU *GET*?
ANYONE WHO THINKS THAT THEY CAN GET A LAUGH OUT OF *THAT* OUGHT TO BE REINCARNATED AS A TOILET PAPER TUBE.
SORRY. I'M ALWAYS LIKE THIS WHEN I'M AT A LOSS FOR WORDS...

SERI-
OUSLY...
SERIOUSLY, HAYATE, YOU'RE SUCH A...
WELL, I HAVE NO CHOICE.
I GUESS I'LL HAVE TO KEEP TAKING CARE OF YOU!!
HUH?

SO, DON'T YOU...
...GO WANDERING OFF, ALL RIGHT?
...
ALL RIGHT!!

YA DID GOOD!!
SLAP
!!

YA STOLE THAT GAG, BUT IT WAS MUCH FUNNIER THAN YER STAGE PERFORMANCE.
OH, SAKUYA-SAN.
NAGI, YA SHOULDN'T LET YERSELF GET DOWN.
CHEER UP AN' I'LL SHOW OFF MY *SPECIAL PERFORMANCE*.

...
YOUR SPECIAL PERFORMANCE?

I CAN DO WITHOUT THAT NAKED STANDUP ROUTINE...
WHO SAID ANYTHIN' ABOUT THAT? THIS IS MUCH MORE AMAZIN'!!

ABOUT...
...HAYATE-KUN?

Episode 6: "Distance—Even if It's Far"

I TOLD YOU I'D BACK YOU UP WITH HAYATE-KUN, BUT...
OH, THIS IS SO AWKWARD.

BETRAYED ME?
YES.

SHEESH...
WHERE HAVE YOU *BEEN*?

HUH?

LAST MONTH, ON THE NIGHT OF MY BIRTHDAY, I WAS ALONE...
...WITH HAYATE-KUN AT THE SCHOOL.

I WANTED
HE GAVE ME A BIRTHDAY PRESENT.
I AM...
SOME LITTLE COOKIES... AND A BIT OF A MEMORY.

THE PRESENT ITSELF WAS JUST AN OBLIGATION GIFT...

...AND I'M SURE THAT'S ALL IT MEANT TO HAYATE-KUN.

BUT AT THAT MOMENT...

...I REALIZED MY TRUE FEELINGS.

I...

...LOVE HAYATE-KUN.

OH.

WELL?
THAT'S IT?

...
SNIFF

...
...

HUH? WHAT DO YOU MEAN, "THAT'S IT?"
I'M BARING MY HEART HERE!!
OKAY, OKAY!! RIGHT!!
SO... WHAT? YOU'RE IN LOVE WITH HIM?
ER... THIS ISN'T QUITE THE REACTION I EXPECTED. SHOULD I START OVER?
NO... I THINK I GET IT.
IT'S JUST THAT YOU HAD SUCH A SERI-OUS TONE IN YOUR VOICE.
I EXPECTED YOU TO SAY...

I'VE BEEN GOING OUT WITH HAYATE-KUN...
...AND I'VE ALREADY DONE BLEEP AND BLEEP WITH HIM!

THAT'S WHAT I THOUGHT, ANYWAY...
WHAT? THERE'S NO WAY THAT WOULD HAPPEN!! WHY WOULD I DO THAT WITH HAYATE-KUN?
UMM... DIDN'T YOU JUST TELL ME YOU LOVED HIM OR SOME-THING?
HOW CAN YOU KEEP SMILING LIKE THAT?
I BETRAYED YOU!!
HA HA... WELL, I GUESS SO...

...BUT I REALIZED SOMETHING WHEN I WENT TO SHIMODA THE OTHER DAY.
WHEN I CONFESSED MY FEELINGS TO HAYATE-KUN...
...I THOUGHT THAT IF HE DIDN'T RETURN THEM...
...I'D NEVER BE ABLE TO SEE HIM AGAIN.
BUT...

...THE TRUTH IS, IF I WANT TO...
...I CAN SEE HIM ANYTIME.
...

IT'S NOT LIKE ONE OF US DIED...

...OR WE HAD SOME BIG FIGHT.
HA HA... SAME ERE.
IT'S FUN TO BE WITH HIM.

HE MAY NOT...
...HAVE FEEL-INGS FOR ME NOW...
...AND MAYBE HE NEVER WILL...

...BUT THAT DOESN'T MEAN WE HAVE TO BE APART.

SO...
...NO MATTER WHO'S IN LOVE WITH HAYATE-KUN...

...SOONER OR LATER...
...I HOPE I'LL BE THE ONE TO WIN HIM. ♡

...

HINAGIKU-SAN, WHY DON'T YOU TELL HIM HOW YOU FEEL?
HUH?
YOU DON'T NEED TO WORRY ABOUT MY FEELINGS.
...

I... DON'T THINK I'LL CONFESS MY LOVE OR ANYTHING LIKE THAT.

WHY NOT?
YOU'RE NOT WORRIED ABOUT *ME*, ARE YOU?

NO... IT'S JUST...
I DON'T KNOW HOW TO PUT IT, BUT...

...IF I TOLD HIM I LOVED HIM FIRST...
...IT'D FEEL LIKE I ***LOST***. IT'D BE DEMEANING.

...

WHAT KIND OF CHILDISH IDEA IS THAT?

WHAT? THIS IS IMPORTANT TO ME!!

OF COURSE, IF ***HE*** CONFESSED TO ***ME***, IT'D BE A DIFFERENT STORY...

...BUT THERE'S NO WAY I'M GOING TO TELL HIM FIRST!!

I DON'T THINK LOVE IS A GAME WHERE YOU WIN OR LOSE...

WELL, THEN.
THIS IS GOING TO BE A COMPETITION, HUH?

WILL I WIN HAYATE-KUN'S HEART...
...OR WILL HAYATE-KUN DECLARE HIS LOVE FOR HINA-SAN?

...
PER-HAPS...

HM?
BOOM

WOW!! INCREDIBLE!
FIREWORKS!!
BUT WHAT ARE THEY FOR?

I BET SOME RICH PEOPLE SOMEWHERE ARE CELEBRATING.
PEOPLE LIKE NAGI-CHAN.
HA HA... YOU MAY BE RIGHT...

WOW!
LAUNCHING ALL THOSE FIREWORKS FOR A BIRTHDAY PARTY...
RICH PEOPLE REALLY **CAN** DO ANYTHING.
IT'S TRUE.
BUT...
KOFF

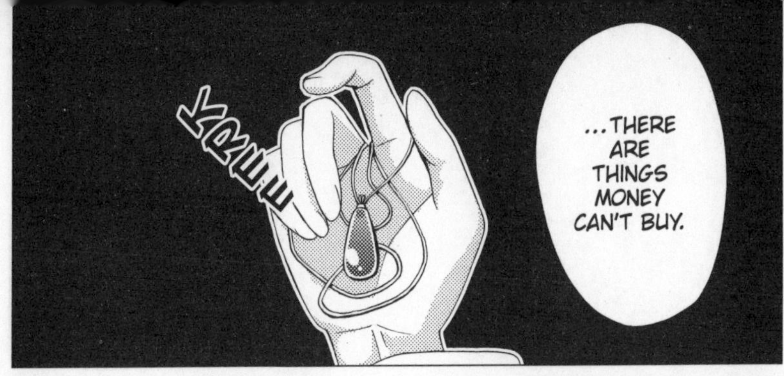

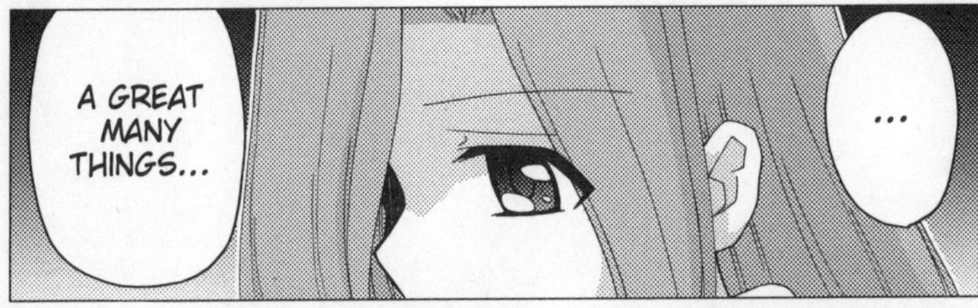

THEY LOOK UP AT THE SAME SKY.

EACH OF THEM...

...STANDS IN A DIFFERENT PLACE...

...BUT FOR NOW THEY'RE ALL LOOKING UP AT THE SAME SKY.

HELLO, MARIA HERE.
TODAY I'LL SHOW YOU HOW TO BREW DELICIOUS TEA.
FIRST HEAT SOME SOFT WATER. PLEASE BE SURE NOT TO USE HARD WATER, BECAUSE THAT WILL SPOIL THE FLAVOR.
TODAY I'M USING ASSAM TEA LEAVES, WHICH ARE THE BEST FOR MILK TEA. PUT TWO GRAMS (ABOUT ONE TEASPOON) PER CUP INTO THE TEAPOT.
POUR THE HOT WATER INTO THE TEAPOT AND WAIT THREE MINUTES. THE TIMING IS IMPORTANT, BECAUSE IF YOU RUSH, NOT ENOUGH OF THE MOST IMPORTANT COMPONENT OF TEA—THE POLYPHENOLIC COMPOUNDS—WILL BE EXTRACTED...
...AND IF YOU WAIT TOO LONG, TOO MUCH WILL BE EXTRACTED, WHICH AFFECTS THE TASTE.
ALL THAT REMAINS IS TO ADD MILK AND SUGAR TO SUIT...
...BRING OUT YOUR FAVORITE TEA CAKES AND ENJOY THEM WITH EVERYONE. ♡ SEE YOU SOON!
WHAT'S THIS?
THIS WAS ONE OF OUR THREE-YEAR ANNIVERSARY COLOR PAGES. ※
※ INDEED IT WAS.

Episode 7: "Hayate Once Upon a Time Story"

Episode 7:
"Hayate Once Upon
a Time Story"

ハヤテのごとく!
Hayate the combat butler

THAT'S MARIA, ISN'T IT?
WELL, A WHOLE LOT HAP-PENED...
HEY!
I'M GOING TO BUY YOU THAT WATCH...
EARN MYSELF FROM A PART-TIME JOB, STARTING TODAY!!
TAAH-DAAH
FIRE-WORKS!!
BUT WHAT ARE THEY FOR?
IN FULL BLOOM!
YES, THEY'RE HANGING IN THERE SURPRISINGLY WELL.
...ON APRIL 3RD.
SO, DON'T YOU

AND THE NEXT DAY...
CHIRP
CHIRP

HAAH
HAAH

...

SHE HAS A COLD.
FWIP FWIP
...
...OJÔ-SAMA SUCCUMBED TO ILLNESS!!
HAAH
HAAH

URGH...
HAAH
THIS IS SO PATHETIC...
HAAH

ER...NO IT ISN'T. OJÔ-SAMA, YOU WORKED REALLY HARD YESTERDAY.
YOU CAN'T HELP GETTING SICK...
YOU SHOULDN'T SPOIL HER SO MUCH.
BUT MARIA-SAN...
ARGH... THIS IS TERRIBLE...

IF I *HAVE* TO GET SICK, IT SHOULD BE AFTER SCHOOL BEGINS, NOT IN THE MIDDLE OF SPRING VACATION! THIS IS THE WASTE OF A GOOD SICK DAY!
NOT EXACTLY ON DEATH'S DOOR, IS SHE?
...
WELL, ANYWAY...

...I'M GOING OUT TO RUN SOME ERRANDS...
...SO PLEASE LOOK AFTER HER, HAYATE-KUN.
GOT IT.

JUST BETWEEN US...
...SHE *REALLY* MUST HAVE PUSHED HERSELF, EH?
HUH?

THANK YOU, HAYATE-KUN.
I'LL LEAVE THE REST TO YOU.
UM... HUH?
HAYATE... HAYATE...
BETTER FOLLOW THAT WEAK VOICE.
AH!! YES, COMING!!

WHAT'S WRONG?
MY THROAT HURTS.
I WANT SOME APPLE JUICE.

GOT IT. I'LL GET YOU SOME RIGHT AWAY.
HAAH
HAAH
OKAY... THANKS...
HEY, WHERE'S MARIA?
FWUP
MARIA-SAN WENT OUT.

...

EGH?
BY THE WAY, KLAUS-SAN IS OUT OF THE HOUSE UNTIL TOMORROW, AND BOTH TAMA AND SHIRANUI ARE AT A PET HOTEL FOR CHECKUPS.

SHIIING
EH?

SHIIING
AH...

OH... I SEE...
TUG
SO...
...WE'RE ALL ALONE.
HUH?

OH NO!
FOR THE FIRST TIME IN AGES I'M ALONE WITH HAYATE...

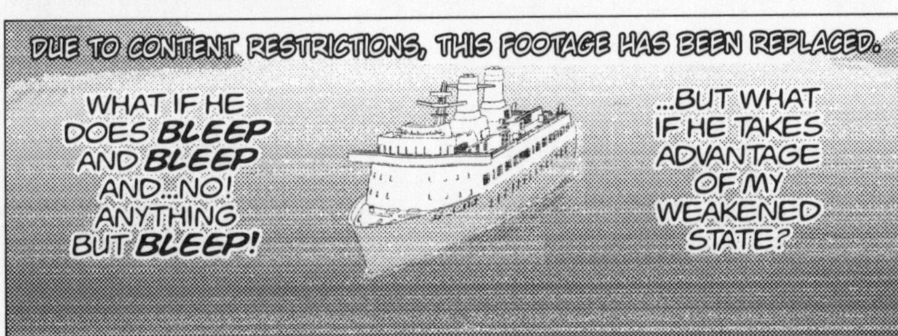
DUE TO CONTENT RESTRICTIONS, THIS FOOTAGE HAS BEEN REPLACED.
...BUT WHAT IF HE TAKES ADVANTAGE OF MY WEAKENED STATE?
WHAT IF HE DOES **BLEEP** AND **BLEEP** AND...NO! ANYTHING BUT **BLEEP!**

SURE, HAYATE IS A GENTLE-MAN...
...BUT MY MOTHER SAID ALL MEN ARE WOLVES IN SHEEP'S CLOTHING.

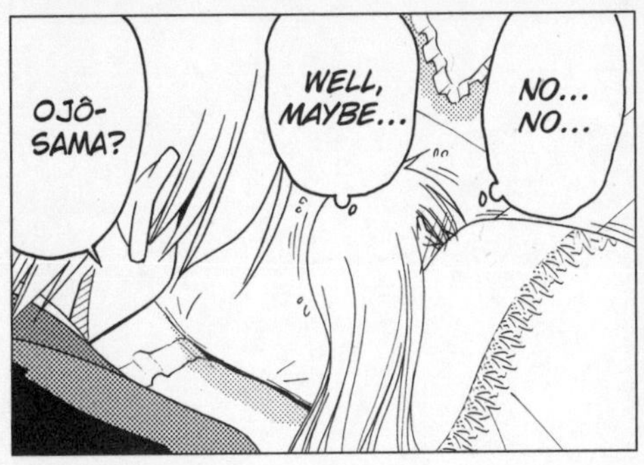
NO... NO...
WELL, MAYBE...
OJÔ-SAMA?

HUH?

TAKE CARE!! I'M OFF!
I'LL JUST BE IN THE NEXT ROOM. IF YOU NEED ANYTHING, PLEASE CALL ME.

WAIT!!

EH? WHAT IS IT?

IT'S GOOD THAT YOU DIDN'T DO ANYTHING... BUT COULDN'T YOU AT LEAST HAVE *CONSIDERED* IT?

HUH?

UM... I MEAN... I'LL BE LONELY ALL BY MYSELF.

EVEN THOUGH I CAN'T GET OUT OF BED, I'M NOT SLEEPY. SO...STAY HERE, OKAY?

BUT WHEN YOU'RE SICK...
...IT'S BEST TO JUST LIE BACK AND GET PLENTY OF REST.

THEN DO SOMETHING TO MAKE ME SLEEPY!!
HMM. SOMETHING TO MAKE YOU SLEEPY?

HOW ABOUT LISTENING TO MY ORIGINAL LULLABY PERFORMED BY MIKU HATSUNE?
MIKKU NIKU NI...♪
THAT THING GOES ON FOREVER!!

THAT'S NOT WHAT I'M TALKING ABOUT!!
ISN'T THERE SOMETHING *ELSE* YOU CAN DO?

AH...
OOG
DON'T GET YOURSELF WORKED UP.

OKAY, THEN... SHALL I READ YOU A STORY?
A STORY?

IT'S A COMMON WAY OF PUTTING SOMEONE TO SLEEP, RIGHT?
URGH ...
YOU'RE TREATING ME LIKE A CHILD AGAIN...
OKAY, OKAY. I'LL PUT UP WITH IT THIS TIME.

JUST PICK AN *ENTERTAINING* ONE.
LEAVE IT TO ME.
ALL RIGHT...
AHEM

...THE SAGA OF DARREN SHAN.
WAIT!!

THAT MANGA IS BASED ON A SERIES THAT'S STILL COMING OUT IN JAPAN, BUT THERE ARE ONLY FOUR PAGES LEFT IN THIS CHAPTER! ARE YOU PLANNING TO GIVE OUT SPOILERS?
BUT IT'S ENTERTAINING ...
NO WAY! YOU CAN'T READ *MAOU, DIVE!* OR *A TALE OF MARI AND THREE PUPPIES AND THE GIANT* FOR THE SAME REASON.
WAS THERE A GIANT IN THAT STORY?

THEN I HAVE NO CHOICE. HOW ABOUT AN OLD STANDARD...
ALICE IN WONDERLAND?
ALICE IN WONDERLAND
RIGHT...NOT SURE IF IT'S A STANDARD IN JAPAN, THOUGH...

UNFORTUNATELY, THE MANGA ARTIST IS ONLY VAGUELY FAMILIAR WITH THIS BOOK.
HUH?

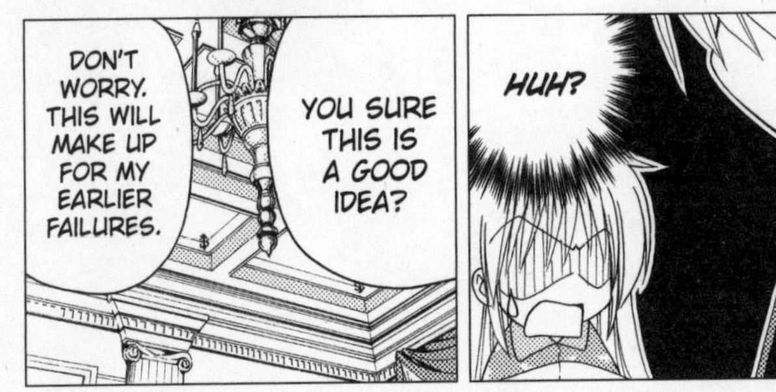
YOU SURE THIS IS A GOOD IDEA?
DON'T WORRY. THIS WILL MAKE UP FOR MY EARLIER FAILURES.

NOW...

SPACE CENTURY 0078...
WHEN ALICE AWOKE, A MYSTERIOUS WORLD STRETCHED OUT BEFORE HER...
IS ALICE GOING TO A BATTLE IN A MO◯LE SUIT?

ER...ANYWAY, ALICE HAD STEPPED INTO WONDERLAND.

ALICE WAS BEWILDERED BY THE SUDDEN TURN OF EVENTS.
WHAT A QUEER PLACE.
I WONDER WHERE I AM...
SHF SHF
SUDDENLY A MYSTERIOUS FIGURE CALLED OUT TO HER.
WELL, WELL, I'VE NEVER SEEN *YOU* AROUND HERE.
HUH?
THEY WERE MAGICAL RABBITS THAT COULD SPEAK.
WE ARE YOUR RABBIT GUIDES.
WOULD YOU LIKE US TO SHOW YOU THE WAY OUT?
TA-DAAH
IT MUST BE ROUGH HAVING TO COVER THE ***CHEESECAKE ANGLE*** FOR OUR ANNIVERSARY STORY.
ALICE SYMPATHIZED.
HEY, IT'S A LIVING!!

THE RABBITS POINTED OUT THE WAY...
GRRM
STOMP
ANYWAY, IF YOU WANT TO REACH THE EXIT, GO THAT WAY!!

...AND IF SHE WANTED TO MAKE ANY PROGRESS, SHE WOULD HAVE TO RUN EVEN FASTER. TRULY A METAPHOR FOR THE ORDEAL OF THE EVERYMAN IN OUR MERCILESS SOCIETY!!
...SO SHE WOULD HAVE TO RUN WITH ALL HER MIGHT JUST TO STAY IN THE SAME PLACE...
IF SHE STOPPED, SHE WOULD MOVE BACKWARDS...
...BUT THE GROUND ITSELF WAS MOVING!!

IF YOU WANT TO REACH THE EXIT, YOU'LL HAVE TO EXCEED YOUR OWN LIMITS!!
GO ON, ALICE!!

SHE THEN BUILT A NEW NATION. IT WAS CALLED THE UNITED STATES OF JAPAN, AND IT IS SAID THAT SHE LIVED THERE IN PEACE...
LATER SHE SLASHED DOWN THE PLAYING CARD SOLDIERS ALL BY HERSELF, BRINGING WONDERLAND UNDER HER CONTROL.
ALICE NEVER HESITATED TO GIVE 110 PERCENT, SO THIS WAS NO ORDEAL AT ALL FOR HER.
BUT BY THE TIME SHE FINISHED SAYING THAT, ALICE WAS LONG GONE.

...HAPPILY EVER AFTER.
THERE'S NOTHING HAPPY ABOUT IT!!!

YOU DIDN'T LIKE THAT?
OF COURSE NOT!!
IT WASN'T HAPPY, AND I WON'T ACCEPT IT!!

I HAVE NO CHOICE, THEN...
...BUT TO USE MY SPECIAL PUNCHLINE...

TO BE CONTIN-UED!!
HUH?
WHETHER THIS WILL ***ACTUALLY*** BE CONTINUED IS STILL IN QUESTION.

Episode 8: "It's a Mystery How a Girl You Didn't Notice at the Beginning of the Term Starts Looking Cute by the End"

APRIL 8TH.
UI-RA
UI-RA
THE START OF A NEW SCHOOL TERM!!

SCHOOL STARTS TODAY, HAYATE-KUN.
YES, I'M FINALLY A JUNIOR.

WITH THE LOVELY WEATHER, IT REALLY FEELS LIKE THE DAWN OF A NEW BEGINNING.
SPARKLE
SPARKLE
I AGREE...

STARTING TODAY, I'LL BE GOING TO SCHOOL WITH YOU AGAIN...

KOFF
HACK
KOFF
KOFF
KOFF
KOFF
HACK
KOFF

KOFF
HACK
AH... WHAT'S WRONG?
MY HEAD FEELS...
AND OH, MY STOMACH IS SO...
KOFF

HACK
HACK
AH... I FEEL DIZZY...
COULD IT BE... A COLD? AM I COMING DOWN WITH A COLD?
...
KOFF
KOFF

Episode 8: "It's a Mystery How a Girl You Didn't Notice at the Beginning of the Term Starts Looking Cute by the End"

SIGH...
A NEW SCHOOL TERM...
I FEEL SO *BLAH*.
HEY, THAT'S NO WAY FOR A TEACHER TO TALK.
WHATEVER. FEELING BLAH IS FEELING BLAH.
I EVEN FEEL BLAH JUST SAYING THE WORD "BLAH."
FROM NOW ON, WE SHOULD MAKE BLINKING THREE TIMES THE UNIVERSAL SIGNAL TO EXPRESS *BLAH*.
BUT EVEN BLINKING IS BLAH, SO I'M GOING TO PASS ON THAT. AHH... I'M SO DOWN...
...

THIS IS FROM THE DIRECTOR ...
...TO YOU, O LAZY ONE.
WHAT'S THIS? MONEY?
CLASS ROSTER
NOPE. IT'S YOUR STUDENT SEATING CHART!!

WHY'RE YOU GIVING THIS TO ME? I DON'T WANT IT...

!
INSTRUCTOR: YUKIJI KATSURA

EH?
INSTRUC-TOR?
RIGHT. FOR THE NEW TERM, YOU'VE BEEN RE-PROMOTED FROM ASSISTANT INSTRUCTOR TO CLASS INSTRUCTOR.

WHOA! SERIOUSLY, KAORU-SAN?
THAT MEANS I'M GETTING A RAISE!!
HONESTLY, ALL YOU THINK ABOUT IS MONEY.
SO WHAT HAPPENED TO MAKIMURA-CHAN? WAS SHE FIRED?
AH, MAKIMURA SENSEI.

I HEARD SHE'S BEING PROMOTED TO HEAD INSTRUCTOR IN CHARGE OF THE ENTIRE GRADE.
I'M A GENIUS, AFTER ALL!
Chief!
ONCE AGAIN, MY JUNIOR HAS BECOME MY SUPERIOR...

...
HANG ON...

I WONDER HOW THE CLASSES HAVE BEEN ASSIGNED.

YOU MEAN WHICH CLASS WE'RE IN?
YES.
I MIGHT BE IN A DIFFERENT CLASS THAN YOU.

HMM...
I DON'T KNOW HOW THEY ASSIGN CLASSES...

...BUT I DON'T THINK THAT'LL HAPPEN...
...FOR CRUCIAL PLOT REASONS.
PLOT REASONS?

WHAT YOU *SHOULD* BE ASKING...
...IS WHO WILL BE IN CLASS WITH US.
YES, I WONDER ...

IF YOU'D LIKE TO KNOW THAT BADLY, SHALL I TELL YOU?
AH, KATSURA SENSEI.

ALL OF YOUR CLASS-MATES ARE LISTED...
...IN THIS REGIS-TRY!

DOES THAT MEAN YOU'RE OUR HOMEROOM TEACHER?
WHAT'S WITH THE FACE?
NEVER MIND. BUT I ADMIT I'M CURIOUS...
...ABOUT WHO WILL BE IN OUR CLASS...

1. ?
Actually a ghost.

2. ?
The daughter of a Shinto priest.

3. ?

4. ?
Wears her hair slicked back.

5. ?
The weakest member of the kendo club.

6. ?

7. ?
Afraid of heights.

8. ?

9. ?

10. ?
Cosplays as a robot.

11. Nagi Sanzenin.

12. ?

13. ?
Grandchild of an appliance chain owner.

14. ?
Shop owner.

15. ?
"Let's Go Onmyouji" girl.

16. ?

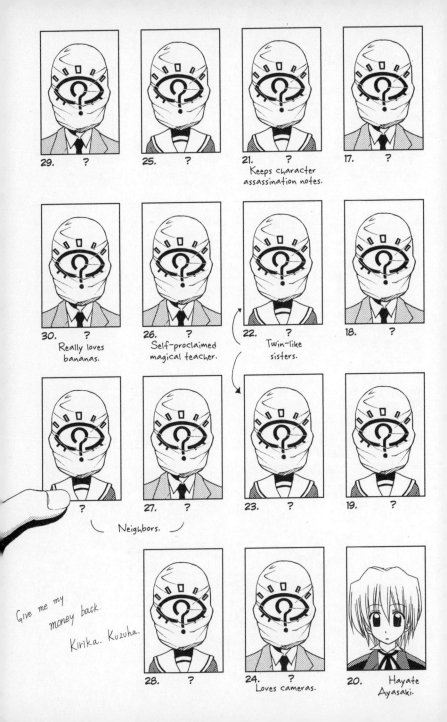

17. ?

18. ?

19. ?

20. Hayate Ayasaki.

21. ?
Keeps character assassination notes.

22. ?
Twin-like sisters.

23. ?

24. ?
Loves cameras.

25. ?

26. ?
Self-proclaimed magical teacher.

27. ?

28. ?

29. ?

30. ?
Really loves bananas.

?

Neighbors.

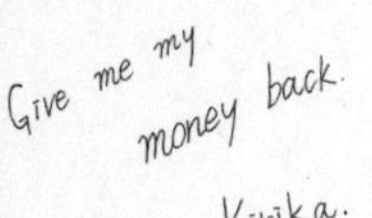
Give me my money back.
Kirika. Kuzuha.

HEY!!
HUH? WHAT?

WHAT KIND OF LAZY CLASS ROSTER *IS* THIS?
CAN'T YOU MAKE SOMETHING MORE THOROUGH, LIKE THAT ***MAGICAL TEACHER*** HAS?
TELL THAT TO THE MAGICAL TEACHER... I MEAN MAKIMURA-CHAN.

SERIOUSLY... JUST ZIP IT...
...AND LET'S GO ON IN.
CHAK

...

IS THIS THE HEAD OFFICE OF THE YUM○TO OR SOME-THING?
I CAN'T TAKE ANY MORE OF THIS...

WELL... ER...

BEING UNABLE TO SEE OUR CLASSMATES' FACES CERTAINLY IS ***CREEPY***.
I HAVE NO IDEA WHAT'S GOING ON.

HA HA... YOU LOOK DIS-TRESSED, HAYATE AYASAKI.
WHO ARE YOU?

YOINK
HA! I'M ONE OF YOUR CLASS-MATES...

...KOTARO AZUMA-MIYA!!

...

SO... WHO ARE YOU?
JUST LIKE KATSUM◯TA-KUN! WHO ARE YOU?
HEY, I'VE BEEN AROUND!! YOU FOUGHT WITH ME AT THE KENDO CLUB. IT'S ME, AZUMAMIYA!!

OH... AZU...
ER...
I GUESS I REMEMBER THAT... MAYBE...
I GET IT!! I GET IT NOW!!
I HAVE TO HELP HIM.
AND EVEN THOUGH AZUMAMIYA-KUN IS THE WEAKEST MEMBER OF THE CLUB...
WA HA HA HA... GOOD, NONO-HARA!!
WAARGH!!
...
?
?

SO WHAT DOES AZU-MAMIYA-KUN, WHOM NONE OF OUR READERS REMEMBER...
...WANT FROM US?
...

AS YOU KNOW...
...I HAD A BUTLER NAMED NONOHARA.
YOU DID?
ER... I *THINK* I REMEMBER HIM...

THE OTHER DAY NONOHARA TOLD ME...
NOW THAT I'VE GRADUATED FROM HIGH SCHOOL...
...I'M GOING TO ENGLAND FOR BUTLER TRAINING.

AND NOW HE'S ***GONE!!***
LEAVING ME ALONE... ALL ALONE...
HE'S LIKE A JILTED LOVER.
I KNOW.
SO? WHAT DOES THAT HAVE TO DO WITH US?
TCH!! YOU STILL DON'T GET IT?
LOOK...
...WHAT I'M TRYING TO SAY IS...

...I'LL ...PERMIT YOU TO BE...
...MY BUTLER!!
PING

HEY, WAIT!
PLEASE...

I'M ALREADY NAGI OJÔ-SAMA'S BUTLER. I CAN'T WORK FOR *YOU* AT THE SAME TIME!!
COME ON, JUST PLACE A "BUTLER WANTED" AD OR CALL A TEMP AGENCY LIKE F◯OMA.
OR HIRE SOMEONE FROM THAT BUTLER CAFÉ IN IKEBUKURO.

WELL, THAT DIDN'T WORK, SO I'M ASKING YOU!!
REALLY?

SO WHY ME?
BECAUSE... BECAUSE...

YOU KNOW ABOUT THE ORIENTATION EVENT, RIGHT? "A FIELD TRIP TO TAKAO MOUNTAIN TO GET ACQUAINTED WITH ALL YOUR CLASSMATES."
THAT'S A SURPRISINGLY *ORDINARY* FIELD TRIP FOR THIS SCHOOL.
WE'RE SUPPOSED TO FORM TEAMS AND CLIMB THE MOUNTAIN TOGETHER...
YAK YAK
YAK YAK
...BUT ...

...I...DON'T HAVE ANY FRIENDS...
...SO I'LL BE ALL BY MYSELF, FEELING ALIENATED.
WHOA...

YOU DON'T WANT TO FEEL ALIENATED...
...SO YOU'RE TRYING TO HIRE A *BUTLER* TO BE YOUR FRIEND.
WELL, I CAN KIND OF UNDERSTAND THAT...
I KNEW YOU WOULD!

THIS IS EXACTLY THE KIND OF CLIQUISH EVENT THAT KEEPS THE LESS *CONVENTIONALLY POPULAR* KIDS AWAY FROM SCHOOL!
YES! SPOKEN LIKE THE QUEEN OF SOCIAL WITHDRAWAL!!
DON'T CALL ME THAT.
BUT...

...I DON'T MIND...
...FEELING ALIENATED.

!!

WHEN I WAS LITTLE THE OTHER KIDS' PARENTS WARNED THEM NOT TO ASSOCIATE WITH THE AYASAKIS' SON, SO I USUALLY ATE LUNCH ALONE.
MY PARENTS REALLY *DID* CAUSE ALL KINDS OF TROUBLE FOR THEM...
...SO I LEARNED TO BE OKAY WITH THAT.
SUCH COURAGE!!
BUT OUR CLASSMATES...

...ARE, YOU KNOW...
HEH HEH HEH
I KNOW...
TO BE CONTINUED FOR REAL THIS TIME...

Episode 9:

"I Want to Go Hiking. I Really Want to Go. I Mean, I Want to Get Out of My Workplace"
MT. TAKAO SUMMIT

HIKING!
IT IS SAID TO BE SUCH A HORRIFYING ORDEAL THAT EVEN THE *DEAD* FEAR IT!!

TO REACH THE MOUNTAIN OF HELL, MT. TAKAO, WHICH TOWERS OVER THE DEVIL CONTINENT OF HACHIOJI...
...A DREADFUL RITUAL WAS HELD IN THE CITY OF TOKYO AGAIN LAST YEAR. A YOUNG MAN MARKED FOR SACRIFICE WAS FORCED TO CARRY A HEAVY CROSS (-STRAPPED BACKPACK) ...A BURDEN SO GREAT HE REGRETTED THAT HE WAS EVER BORN.

THE SCENE TERRIFIED ALL WHO SAW IT.
AS THEY LOOKED UPON THE HORRIBLE SIGHT, THEY COULD ONLY WEEP!!

WHY MUST SUCH A CRUEL RITUAL TAKE PLACE IN THIS DAY AND AGE?
IN THE CIVILIZED WORLD OF TODAY, WHAT MEANING DOES IT HOLD?

PONDER THE MEANING OF IT ALL YOU LIKE...
...BUT IT *IS* A SCHOOL EVENT, SO YOU NEED TO GO.

...
...
...

HIKING... IF YOU PARTICIPATE, YOUR VERY **SOUL** WILL BE FORFEIT...
URK
I WON'T ALLOW YOU TO SKIP SCHOOL! THE NEW TERM HAS JUST BEGUN!
JUST ABOUT EVERYONE WHO GREW UP IN TOKYO CLIMBED THAT MOUNTAIN AS A STUDENT...
...SO IT'S NOT REALLY ALL THAT FORMIDABLE.

YOU SHOULDN'T GO ALONG WITH SOMETHING JUST BECAUSE EVERYONE IS DOING IT!!
EVEN THOSE JAPAN ADVERTISING COUNCIL PSAS SAY SO!!!
DON'T TRY TO PUT THE MORAL DECISIONS OF YOUNG PEOPLE ON THE SAME LEVEL AS HIKING.

YOU GOT SICK THE OTHER DAY DUE TO YOUR LACK OF ENDURANCE!!
GO CLIMB THAT MOUNTAIN AND TRY TO BUILD A LITTLE PHYSICAL STRENGTH!!

IF I TRY TO CLIMB THAT MOUNTAIN, I'LL DIE BEFORE I BUILD ANY STRENGTH.
YOU WON'T DIE!!
Hayate-kun, don't spoil her!!
JUMPING FORWARD A BIT...
...IT'S NOW APRIL 10TH, THE DAY OF THE HAKUOU GAKUIN SCHOOL ORIENTATION HIKING TRIP TO MT. TAKAO.

ATTENTION, PLEASE.

YEESH... ENOUGH ALREADY.

BEFORE WE START CLIMBING MT. TAKAO, THERE ARE SOME IMPORTANT THINGS TO KEEP IN MIND.
MT. TAKAO
FIRST OF ALL, LISTEN UP!!
DON'T TAKE MOUNTAIN CLIMBING LIGHTLY!!
EVEN THOUGH IT'S JUST MT. TAKAO, ACCI-DENTS GO HAND IN HAND WITH MOUNTAIN CLIMBING!!
IF YOU DON'T TAKE THIS SERIOUSLY, YOU'RE GOING TO GET HURT!!

GOT IT? THIS MOUNTAIN IS TREACHEROUS!! *TREACHEROUS!!*
SO DON'T BE NEGLIGENT! BE PREPARED!
THIS COMING FROM THE WOMAN IN A MINISKIRT AND HIGH HEELS...
IS SHE REALLY GOING TO CLIMB THE MOUNTAIN IN THAT OUTFIT?

OKAY, THIS WILL BE A GROUP ACTIVITY ORGANIZED INTO TEAMS. LINE UP WITH YOUR TEAM...
...AND PROCEED IN ORDER!!

ALLOW ME TO EXPLAIN A FEW THINGS ABOUT MT. TAKAO.

MT. TAKAO IS JUST UNDER 600 METERS IN HEIGHT. IT'S A VERY POPULAR MOUNTAIN IN TOKYO.

THE PATHS ARE EASY TO CLIMB AND VERY SAFE, SO IT'S OFTEN CHOSEN AS A SPOT FOR GRADE SCHOOL FIELD TRIPS.

IN SHORT, THIS MOUNTAIN IS PERFECT FOR CASUAL HIKING!!

THAT'S A LIE!!!
I'M DYING OUT HERE!!
WE ONLY JUST STARTED.
I CAN'T BELIEVE YOU REFUSED TO CARRY MY PACK FOR ME.
BUT MARIA-SAN SAID...
LATELY I THINK YOU'VE BEEN SPOILING NAGI, HAYATE-KUN.
EH? HAVE I?
IT'S TRUE SHE'S ON THE DELICATE SIDE, BUT IF YOU DO EVERYTHING FOR HER SHE'LL LOSE WHAT LITTLE STRENGTH SHE HAS.
WELL, THAT'S TRUE.
THAT'S WHY I WANT YOU TO MAKE SURE...
...THAT NAGI CARRIES HER BACKPACK ALL THE WAY UP.

URGH... THAT MARIA... WHO DOES SHE THINK SHE IS?
MARIA-SAN IS HONESTLY CONCERNED ABOUT YOU, OJÔ-SAMA.

IT'S NOT FAIR!!
EVEN THOUGH I'M A DELICATE FLOWER...

...I'M STILL CARRYING MORE THAN *THAT* GUY!!
CLASSMATE 1 AZUMAMIYA-KUN
...
UMM... AZUMA-MIYA-SAN...
...ARE YOU ALL RIGHT?

HMPH.
JUST FURTHER PROOF THAT RICH, PAMPERED OBOCCHAMA ARE NO GOOD.

WHAT ARE YOU DOING HERE, KOTETSU-SAN?
CLASSMATE 2 KOTETSU-KUN
WHAT A SILLY QUESTION, AYASAKI.
WE'RE BUDDIES ON THE SAME TEAM, IN THE SAME CLASS.
IS THAT SO?

SO, HAYATA-KUN... WHAT ARE YOU GOING TO DO ABOUT AZUMAMIYA-KUN?
CLASSMATE 3 IZUMI-SAN
WELL, WE HAVE TO MOVE IN TEAMS, SO WE CAN'T LEAVE HIM HERE.
HE'LL HAVE TO GET UP AND WALK SOMEHOW.

HA... HA HA...
A SHORTCUT...
HUH?
A SHORTCUT...

I CAN'T GO ON CLIMBING THIS MOUNTAIN PATH!!
VOOM
I'M TAKING A SHORTCUT!!

YAAAAAH!!
WSST
YOU STUPID MOUNTAIN!
AHH!!
WAIT!! AZUMAMIYA-SAN!!

HAYATE!! IF WE DON'T STOP HIM OUR TEAM WILL FALL APART!!
HURRY UP AND GET HIM!! I'LL REST HERE!!
GOT IT.
WAIT!! I'M GOING WITH YOU!!

...

THAT'S AN OBVIOUS FLAG...
...FOR WHAT'S GOING TO HAPPEN NEXT.
HUH?

WE WON'T LOSE OUR WAY EASILY.

ARE YOU SURE, ISUMI?
YES.

GOING STRAIGHT ON A MOUNTAIN PATH LIKE THIS...
...MAKES IT MORE DIFFICULT TO GET LOST, WATARU-KUN.
CHING

BUT I THINK WE'VE MANAGED IT ANYWAY.
OH?
...

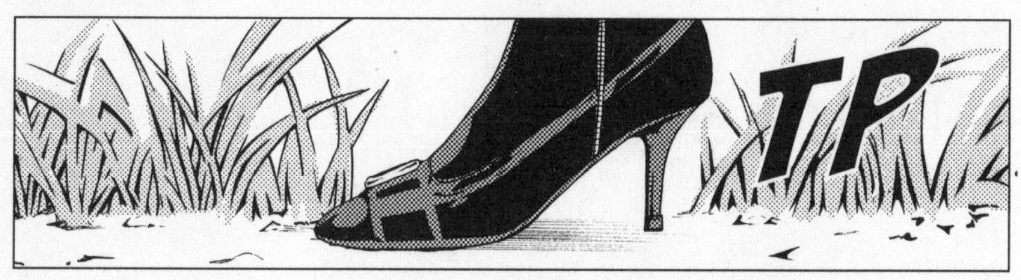
TP

HEY, YUKIJI.
HUH?
WHAT?

HOW CAN YOU CLIMB A MOUNTAIN IN HIGH HEELS LIKE IT'S NOTHING?
OH, MAYBE BECAUSE THEY'RE NAME BRAND.
They were pretty expensive, you know.

THE POWER OF THE FOOL IS AN ASTONISH-ING THING.
WHY'D YOU DECIDE TO GO HIKING IN THAT OUTFIT ANYWAY?

IT'S ILLEGAL FOR A WOMAN IN HER LATE 20S TO WEAR UNFASHION-ABLE CLOTHES IN PUBLIC.
NOW STOP WASTING YOUR BREATH AND WALK, WALK, WALK! WE'RE IN LAST PLACE!
URGH...

HEY, YUKI-CHAN!!
HM?
WHAT?
AYASAKI-KUN AND HIS TEAM ARE MISSING?

ISUMI-SAN AND HER GROUP ARE MISSING ON OUR SIDE TOO.
HEY, C'MON... HOW COULD THEY GET LOST IN A PLACE LIKE MT. TAKAO?

WELL, KNOWING THEM, THEY CAN FEND FOR THEMSELVES IF SOMETHING HAPPENS...
MAYBE BEING DEMOTED TO ASSISTANT INSTRUCTOR WON'T BE ENOUGH THIS TIME.
WE NEED TO FIND THEM RIGHT AWAY.

I HAVE NO CHOICE.

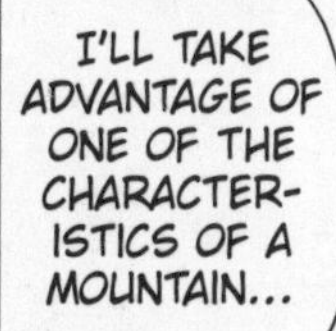
I'LL TAKE ADVANTAGE OF ONE OF THE CHARACTERISTICS OF A MOUNTAIN...

HINA'S EMBARRASSING PAST, PART ONE!!
WHEN SHE WAS 10 YEARS OLD...

WHAM

WHAT WERE YOU PLANNING TO ECHO ALL OVER THE MOUNTAIN, ONEE-CHAN?
YOU GOT HERE FASTER THAN THE ECHO, HINA.

HUH?
MISSING?

THEY'VE GONE TRAGICALLY ASTRAY, HINA.
YES, YOU COULD SAY THEY'VE WANDERED DOWN THE WRONG PATH.
I'M NOT SENSING A LOT OF URGENCY FROM YOU PEOPLE.
ANYWAY, HINA...
...I'LL LEAVE THIS GROUP TO YOU WHILE WE FIND THE MISSING PERSONS.

WE?
ER...
YOU MEAN US?

LET'S GO, MS. CLASS REP!!
HUH? WAIT!! WHY ME?
OWW
WAIT!! ONEE-CHAN!!
THIS IS A FLAG THAT WE'RE GOING TO GET LOST.
LOOKS LIKE THERE ARE BEARS AROUND TOO.
BEWARE OF BEARS!!
...

WHERE ARE WE?

WE'RE FINALLY ALONE TOGETHER.

ARE YOU BOTH IDIOTS?

NEVER MIND!!

WE SHOULDN'T DAWDLE HERE. LET'S GET BACK TO THE OTHERS...

SNAP

HM?

"SNAP"?

ISN'T THIS MT. TAKAO?
IT'S SUPPOSED TO BE...

YAAAAH!!
AND THIS IS WHY...
I HOPE THEY'VE REACHED THE PEAK BY NOW!
...WE'LL HAVE TO CONTINUE IN THE NEXT CHAPTER.

Episode 10:
"A Child Is a Lost Child
Because He's Lost.
I'm Lost in Life. H-E-L-P..."

AN ANACONDA ESCAPED INTO THE TOKYO AREA THE OTHER DAY...
GIANT BEAR APPEARS!!
MAOKO KOTANI
...BUT NOW WE'VE DISCOVERED THAT THE SAME MAN ALLOWED A **BEAR** TO ESCAPE AS WELL.

THE BEAR IS EXTREMELY VICIOUS, AND WE HAVE NOT YET FOUND...
...

MY GOOD-NESS!
I HOPE THEY'RE ALL RIGHT...
...

WELL, I DOUBT A VICIOUS BEAR THAT ESCAPED IN TOKYO...
...COULD HAVE WANDERED UP MT. TAKAO...
...AND SOMEHOW ENDED UP FINDING THE STUDENTS AND ATTACKING THEM. NO, THERE'S NO WAY SUCH AN UNFORTUNATE SET OF CIRCUM-STANCES COULD POSSIBLY OCCUR. ♡
HEH

UWAAAH !!

WHAT *IS* THAT MONSTER?

DON'T ASK ME!!

TMP TMP

WHY IS IT ATTACK-ING US?

I'M TELLING YOU, I DON'T KNOW!!

TMP TMP TMP

BY THE WAY, WHERE'S AZUMA-MIYA?

HUH?

I HOPE HE ISN'T TRYING TO AVOID ATTACK BY THE DISCRED-ITED METHOD...

...OF PLAYING DEAD!

I'M DEAD.

...
...
C'mon, I'm dead ...

HE'S ASKING THE BEAR TO READ IT.
AND BELIEVE WHAT HE READS.

HSSSSSSS!!
YEEEK!!

DON'T MESS AROUND! *RUN!!*

SHUMP

UMM... NEE-CHAN, ARE YOU ALL RIGHT?

HUH?

HEH... I'M OKAY.

I'VE BEEN FEELING PRETTY GOOD THESE DAYS...

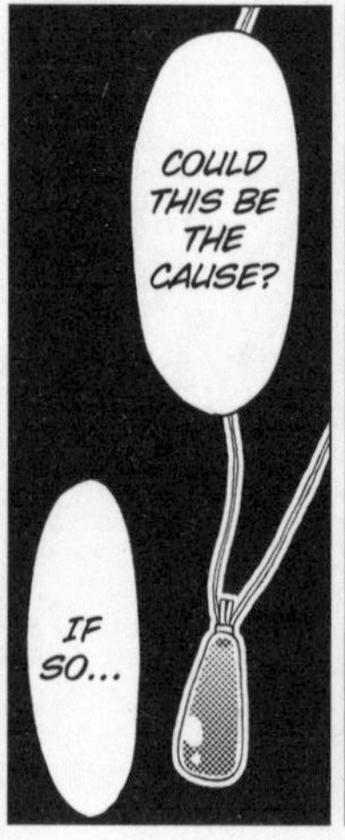

HUH?

YEEK!!
FWUMP

WH... WHAT...

THERE'S NO SENSE PUSHING YOURSELF.
LET'S TAKE A LITTLE BREAK.
BUT...

I SHOULD HAVE BEEN LEADING THE WAY.
THIS ALWAYS HAPPENS WITH ISUMI.

I'M SORRY YOU GOT INVOLVED IN THIS.
NO, NOT AT ALL.

IN FACT, THIS IS ALL MY...
UM...

BY THE WAY, WHERE *IS* ISUMI-SAN?
LIKE I SAID...
...SHE'S LOST AS USUAL.

BUT WHAT ARE WE GOING TO DO ABOUT THAT ***BEAR***?
DON'T ASK ME...
RAWR

ALL WE CAN DO FOR NOW IS JUST LEAVE IT BE.
I SUPPOSE YOU'RE RIGHT.

WHAT A MESS... I NEED TO GET BACK TO OJÔ-SAMA.
I DON'T MIND THIS SITUATION ONE BIT.
HOW'D YOU LIKE TO BE *BEAR BAIT?*

SHOOF
WELL, IT'S BEST NOT TO MOVE AT THIS POINT.
WE JUST HAVE TO BE VERY, VERY PATIENT...
IF YOU THINK IT'S BEST NOT TO MOVE, STOP MOVING OVER HERE!!

IT'S UNCOMFORTABLE LEANING AGAINST THIS BRANCH! I WAS JUST GOING TO SCOOT OVER A BIT...
FORGET IT! JUST STAY PUT!!
SHF
NOW, NOW, DON'T SAY THAT...
YOU IDIOT!! STAY BACK!!
SHF
COME ON, JUST A LITTLE KISS...
ARE YOU CRAZY? THIS HAS *DEATH* WRITTEN ALL OVER IT!!
IN A CLICHÉ SETUP LIKE THIS, ONE OF US IS BOUND TO FALL OUT OF—
OOF
OH NO!! *UWAAAH!!*

...

HISSS !!

YEEP!!

OW!!

BUT...

...I CAN'T DO ANYTHING BY MYSELF...

GROWWWWL!!

YEEK!!

I DON'T THINK SO!!

AYASAKI!!
COME ON, HURRY!!
WE'RE GETTING OUT OF HERE TOGETHER!!

A...
AYASAKI...
PLIP
AYASAKI!!
HUG
ARGH!! SAVE IT FOR LATER!
!!
HISSSS!

AYASAKI!!

SLASH

CHIRP CHIRP

SONTORY
PLIP

LET'S GET GOING. WE CAN'T CATCH UP WITH THE OTHERS IF WE DON'T START WALKING.
YES... OKAY.

HERE, TAKE THIS.
!

HUH? BUT THIS IS...
IT'S JUST WATER. YOU DON'T WANT TO WEAR YOURSELF OUT AGAIN.

...
NO, IT'S JUST THAT...

WHAT? IT'S IMPORTANT TO STAY HYDRATED.
IT'S BEST TO DRINK SOME EVEN IF YOU DON'T FEEL THIRSTY.

BUT...
...YOUR LIPS... TOUCHED ...
?
SO WHAT?

IF YOU'RE NOT GOING TO TAKE CARE OF YOURSELF, FORGET IT.
SEE YOU LATER, NEE-CHAN.
HUH?

GEEZ!!
PLIP

WAIT, WATARU-KUN!

MEAN-WHILE...
HFF
HFF

WHEN THIS IS OVER I'M GOING TO BUY THIS MOUNTAIN AND LEVEL IT TO THE GROUND.
SOUNDS GOOD.
DON'T LET THE RAGE CONSUME YOU.
HFF
HFF
HFF
...THE HIKE CONTINUES.
DO YOU KNOW THAT SAYING, "THE MUMMY HUNTER BECOMES THE MUMMY"?
DON'T TELL ME WE'RE LOST TOO!
EEEK
?

Episode 11:
"A Wild Life. Animals Are Unforgiving to Me"

...TO MY AYASAKI?
?
WHY ME? UGH!
OW

WHY ARE YOU HITTING ME?
TUP
IF YOU'RE GOING TO FIGHT, FIGHT THE BEAR!!
OH!! AYASAKI!!

I'M GLAD YOU'RE OKAY.
DO I LOOK OKAY TO YOU?
YOU LOOK LIKE YOU'RE READY FOR A LITTLE HURT/COMFORT.
YOU ALREADY TOOK CARE OF THE "HURT."
BLUP BLUP
URGH... YOU'RE WEARING ME OUT, YOU ID...
FWUMP
ARE YOU ALL RIGHT?

I HAVE NO CHOICE.
!!
WHUP

WAIT!! PUT ME DOWN!!
SHH!! HE'S LOST INTEREST IN US! DON'T STRUGGLE!

COME ON, WE'RE GETTING OUT OF HERE NOW!!
ER... OKAY!!

BUT WHY'D THE BEAR STOP ATTACKING US?

I DON'T KNOW, BUT I'M NOT COM-PLAINING.

LET'S GET AWAY WHILE HE'S DISTRACTED!!
OKAY!!
...

Episode 11:
"A Wild Life, Animals Are Unforgiving to Me"

BREATHING DEEP THE FRESH AIR OF THE FOREST...

FEELING YOUR MIND CLEANSED BY THE WOODLAND FLOWERS BUDDING IN THE SPRING...
LETTING YOUR THOUGHTS DRIFT INTO THE REFRESHING BLUE SKY...

DON'T YOU THINK FEELINGS LIKE THESE...

...ARE THE REAL THRILL OF MOUNTAIN CLIMBING?

NO, WE DON'T.

HFF

HFF

I SEE...

BUT OBSESSING OVER HOW TOUGH IT IS TO CLIMB JUST MAKES IT FEEL EVEN *TOUGHER*.
SINCE YOU'VE GOT TO CLIMB IT ANYWAY, YOU MIGHT AS WELL THINK ABOUT SOMETHING ENJOYABLE.
...?!
SOMETHING ENJOY-ABLE?

GEE, I'M REALLY SORRY.
MT. TAKAO
I'M SORRY ABOUT MAKING YOU GO THROUGH SUCH HARDSHIP.

YOU'RE AWFUL!! YOU SHOULD NEVER HAVE BECOME SUCH A DIFFICULT MOUNTAIN TO CLIMB!!
BOW BOW
I'M SORRY. IT WAS A FOOLISH IMPULSE. FROM NOW ON I'LL BE A LEVEL PLAIN, SO PLEASE FORGIVE ME.
MT. TAKAO
NO! I'LL NEVER FORGIVE YOU! INSTEAD OF A PLAIN, TURN INTO A DOWNSLOPE RIGHT NOW!
I WILL DEFINITELY CONSIDER YOUR SUGGESTION, BUT RIGHT NOW I...
MT. TAKAO
I DON'T KNOW WHAT YOU'RE THINKING ABOUT NOW, BUT TRY TO STAY POSITIVE.

OKAY, LET'S THINK UP SOME NEW GU◯DAM FANFIC COUPLINGS...
IS THAT THE SORT OF THING YOU SHOULD THINK ABOUT WHILE COMMUNING WITH NATURE?
POP
WHAT'S SO FUN ABOUT NATURE?
IT'S FUN BECAUSE... WELL...
AH!!!

POP

AWWW...

A TANUKI!! IT'S A TANUKI!!
A BABY TANUKI!!

AIEE! SO CUTE! ♡
I SHOULDN'T TOUCH HIM, RIGHT?
SERIOUSLY, HE'S *SO CUTE!!*

ZOOM
AW!! HE'S RUNNING AWAY!!
HE'S GOING UP THE MOUNTAIN PATH!!
LET'S CHASE HIM!!
HUH?

...
TMP
TMP
TMP

FOR SOME REASON THEY'VE SUDDENLY FOUND THEIR STRENGTH.
SO IT SEEMS.

WE SHOULD HURRY UP...
...AND CHASE THE TANUKI TOO.
HUH?
ER... YES. YOU'RE RIGHT.

YUP.

ANIMALS SURE ARE DANGER-OUS.
SNIFF
SNIFF
I WAS SO SCARED... SO SCARED...

WHEN I FINALLY FOUND AYASAKI-KUN AND THE OTHERS, I DIDN'T EXPECT TO FIND A **BEAR** TOO.
HISSSS!
WE WERE ALMOST EATEN.

HONESTLY... THE NEW TERM HAS ONLY JUST BEGUN, AND THEY'RE ALREADY GETTING INTO TROUBLE.

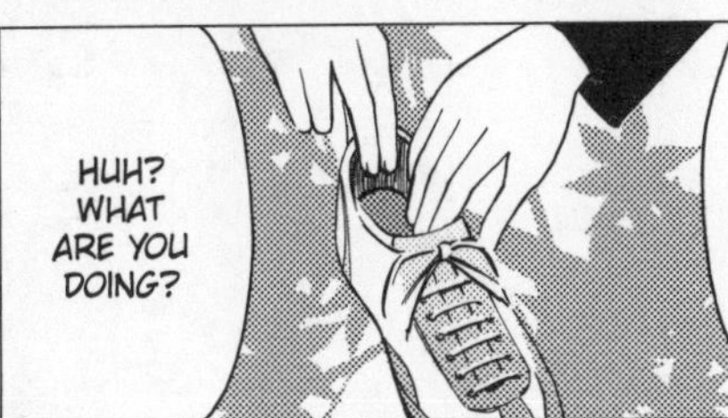
I HAVE NO CHOICE. CLASS REP, YOU STAY HERE. ALSO, IT'S TOUGH TO WALK IN HEELS, SO LEND ME YOUR SHOES.
HUH? WHAT ARE YOU DOING?

WHAT DO YOU THINK?
I **AM** THEIR TEACHER, AFTER ALL.

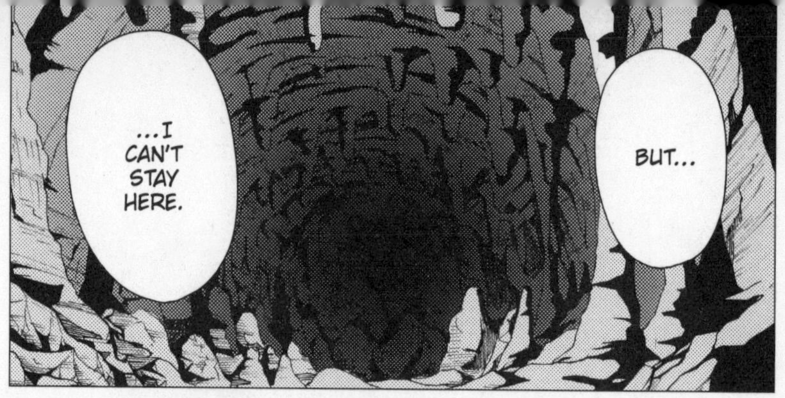

...YOU'RE GOING TO...

...FIGHT THAT THING?

YOU CAN'T!!

THAT'S ABSURD!!

ABSURD OR NOT...

...I DON'T HAVE ANY CHOICE.
CLAW CLAW
...

WE'RE IN TROUBLE.
YES INDEED.
...

WE'VE DROPPED FAR BEHIND.

I HOPE WE CAN CATCH UP TO THE OTHERS BY NOON.
ME TOO.

BUT WHAT ABOUT ISUMI-SAN?
I THINK SHE'S STILL LOST.
HMPH... DON'T SWEAT IT.

THAT'S TYPICAL OF ISUMI.
BESIDES ...
...ISUMI ISN'T AS FRAGILE AS SHE LOOKS.
SPRING WATER

...
I SEE.

IS THAT WHAT YOU LIKE ABOUT HER?
!!
SPLURT
WHA-WHA-WHA...WHAT ARE YOU SAYING?
ARE YOU IMPLYING THAT I...IT'S NOT LIKE THAT!!!
I SEE...

WELL, IF YOU DON'T LIKE HER, THAT'S OKAY TOO.
I...I DIDN'T SAY I DON'T LIKE HER!!

OKAY, OKAY. SO LET'S JUST SAY YOU'RE **AMBIVALENT** ABOUT HER.
WHAT'S WITH THAT NONCHALANT ATTITUDE? YOU'RE GETTING ON MY NERVES!!!

SHEESH !!
IF YOU'RE GOING TO ACT LIKE THIS, I WON'T HELP YOU ANYMORE... NO MATTER WHAT!!

WELL, WELL.
YOU'RE NOT GOING TO HELP ME, NO MATTER WHAT.

IN THAT CASE, I REALLY AM...
!

HISSS!!

YAAH!!

NEE-CHAN, HURRY!!

B-BUT WHAT'S A BEAR DOING ON MT. TAKAO?

AIEEE!!

DON'T YOU LAY A FINGER ON MY STUDENTS!!

SENSEI !!

HURRY UP AND GET OUT OF HERE, YOU TWO!!

DON'T WORRY.

SKTCH

TO BE CONTINUED

BONUS STORY

MARIA-SAN'S WHITE DAY ♥

BUT NOW THAT I'M ACTUALLY GIVING IT TO HIM, I FEEL A LITTLE SHY.
I SHOULD DO A LITTLE PRACTICE RUN.
MEW?
?

HERE, HAYATE-KUN.
PLEASE ACCEPT THESE HOMEMADE COOKIES IN RETURN FOR YOUR VALENTINE'S CHOCOLATES. ♡

...
...
OR WILL HE TAKE THAT AS A SUBTLE LOVE MES-SAGE?

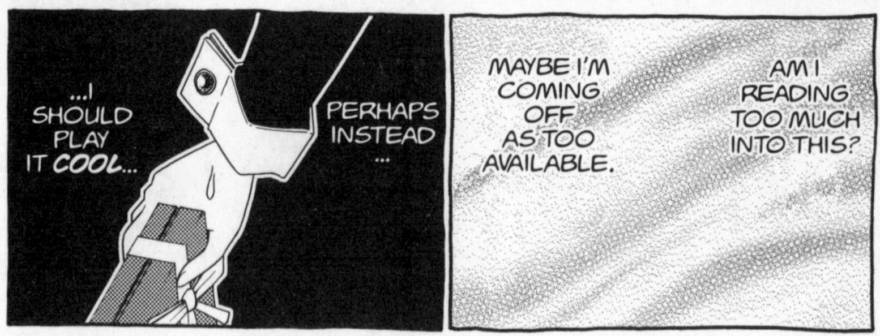
AM I READING TOO MUCH INTO THIS?
MAYBE I'M COMING OFF AS TOO AVAILABLE.
PERHAPS INSTEAD ...
...I SHOULD PLAY IT COOL...

IT'S NOT LIKE I MADE THESE FOR YOU, HAYATE-KUN!!

...
...

THIS ISN'T WORKING... IT'S LIKE THAT TREND, *TSUN*-SOMETHING.
I MEAN, IT'S SENDING AN EVEN ***STRONGER*** LOVE MESSAGE THAN BEFORE! HOW FORMIDABLE THIS *TSUN*-SOMETHING IS!!
THIS IS NO GOOD...
IF I ACT DIFFERENTLY FROM NORMAL, I'LL JUST DIG MYSELF IN DEEPER.

I SHOULD GO BACK TO THE BASICS.
HOW DO OTHER PEOPLE DO THIS? MUST THINK...
HAYATE-KUN!!

I LOVE YOU.
HUH?

...
...
MEW?

I...I...I DIDN'T MEAN YOU, HAYATE-KUN! ER...WHAT I MEAN IS... I WAS JUST TALKING TO SHIRANUI!!
AH!! ER... I SEE!! GEEZ...YOU REALLY SURPRISED ME!!
O-OF COURSE!! HERE, HAYATE-KUN, YOU CAN HAVE THESE COOKIES I WAS GOING TO GIVE TO SHIRANUI!!
HEY...ARE YOU A *TSUNDERE?*
NO, I'M NOT!!
HEY.
THIS STORY BELONGS IN VOLUME 12.
MEW?
WHY NOW?
SO ENDS THE INCIDENT OF THE NIGHT OF MARCH 14TH.

HOW DID YOU LIKE *HAYATE THE COMBAT BUTLER* VOLUME 14?

READING IT OVER AGAIN, THERE WERE TOO MANY MULTI-CHAPTER STORIES. AS THE AUTHOR, THAT GAVE ME A LOT TO THINK ABOUT. I SWEAR THE NEXT VOLUME WILL CONTAIN MORE ONE-SHOT STORIES THAT ARE EASIER TO GET THROUGH. I HOPE YOU'LL ENJOY THEM.

ALSO, FOR SOME REASON THIS VOLUME HAD FOUR PAGES LEFT OVER AT THE END. I DREW A NEW ONE-SHOT STORY TO FILL THE SPACE. FRANKLY, DESPITE THEIR APPEARANCE, THE GAG STRIPS AND CHARACTER PROFILES I USUALLY INCLUDE TO FILL OUT A VOLUME REQUIRE A RIDICULOUS AMOUNT OF TIME TO PRODUCE, AND I SIMPLY DIDN'T HAVE THE TIME TO DRAW ANY FOR VOLUME 14. SORRY...

BUT IT GOES AGAINST MY PERSONAL PRINCIPLES TO DO A SECOND-CLASS JOB ON THE BONUS PAGES, SO I REWORKED A LONGER STORY THAT HAD BEEN REJECTED INTO A FOUR-PAGE SHORT STORY AND RAN THAT.

I HAVE QUITE A FEW *HAYATE* STORIES FROM THE LAST FEW YEARS THAT WEREN'T USED FOR ONE REASON OR ANOTHER. IF THIS STORY TURNS OUT TO BE POPULAR, I'D LIKE TO INCLUDE SOME MORE IN FUTURE VOLUMES.

"MARIA-SAN'S WHITE DAY" WAS SOMETHING I MENTIONED ON MY WEBSITE A WHILE BACK, BUT I DIDN'T GET AROUND TO DRAWING IT UNTIL NOW. THOSE WHO DON'T REMEMBER WHAT ELSE HAPPENED ON WHITE DAY CAN GO BACK AND READ VOLUME 12. FOR THOSE WHO DON'T HAVE THAT VOLUME, MAYBE YOU'LL CONSIDER BUYING IT...

WELL, I'M DONE PLUGGING MY WORK, AND THIS IS GETTING PRETTY LONG, SO I'D BETTER END IT HERE.

PLEASE ENJOY THE NEXT VOLUME TOO. AND THE ANIME IS ON TV, SO I HOPE YOU TAKE A LOOK AT THAT AS WELL.☆

BYE NOW! ☆

THE SANZENIN FAMILY'S NEW SECRET!

IN THE UNNECESSARILY HUGE SANZENIN MANSION, BEHIND A MYSTERIOUS DOOR WE'VE FORGOTTEN TO MENTION UNTIL NOW, THERE'S A GIANT UNDERGROUND FACILITY...

BOTH OF US IN SWIMSUITS?
YOU'RE STILL TOO YOUNG FOR THAT, HAYATE!!
KLIK
WE DON'T WANT TO GET YOUR HOPES UP, BUT YOU CAN'T MISS THE NEXT VOLUME!!
VOLUME 15 COMING IN JUNE 2010!!

Working Man

Forced-to-Work Man